JOHNNY REVOLTA'S SHORT CUTS TO BETTER GOLF

by JOHNNY REVOLTA

and CHARLES B. CLEVELAND

Illustrated by JERRY GIBBONS

THOMAS Y. CROWELL COMPANY · NEW YORK

THIS BOOK I dedicate to the game of golf and to the people who play and love the sport. It is also a tribute to Hank Dettlaff, professional at Oshkosh, Wisconsin. When I was thirteen years old, he thought he saw promise in my game. He took me to all the pro tournaments and helped me in the days when I was learning the game. Now I wish to repay, in part, that debt by helping others—as he helped me—to play better golf.

INTRODUCTION BY ELLSWORTH VINES

AFTER WINNING the world's tennis championship, amateur and professional, I gave up the game to turn to golf. I had played for a number of years for fun and shot a pretty respectable game. But it wasn't good enough for the money circuit and when I turned golf pro in 1942, I had to improve my score.

I picked Johnny Revolta to help me, particularly with my short shots. He is known among the pros as the "Iron Master" and he did much to help my game around the greens. But his teachings are also sound for all phases of golf.

Johnny not only is a great player himself, but—in my opinion— is one of the best instructors in the game. He has made a thorough study of golf during his many years as a professional and he knows and understands its special problems.

During the several summers he worked with me after I became a pro, I watched him instruct many other students—beginners, duffers, good and expert players. He has the rare knack of putting across his instruction in clear, unmistakable fashion that is helpful to all golfers.

A good instructor not only must show you how to play the game, but must aid you in overcoming your golf faults. I had trouble with my posture when I came to Johnny, but he helped straighten out that fault.

From my experience, I feel sure he can help you correct your errors and improve your game.

I strongly endorse Johnny Revolta's system. His formula for simplifying the golf swing to a few basic fundamentals is excellent. I believe it helps you pick up the game much more quickly, more easily, and more thoroughly.

I am glad—as one of the thousands of golfers who have studied with Johnny—to have this opportunity to recommend his course of instruction. We found it excellent; I am sure you will too.

BEFORE TEEING OFF IN THIS BOOK

In writing this book, I have followed the system that has been tried, tested, and proved by thousands of pupils.

* * *

It is not my intention to teach you good golf simply by your reading the words of the chapters. Rather, I have prepared the book in the style of the lessons exactly as I give them at the Evanston Golf Club. This is a *work* book. To get the best results, have your set of clubs handy as you read.

* * *

As I make a point, take your clubs out and practice the lesson. Read slowly, trying out each bit of information.

* * *

Pretend, as you read, that I am talking to you out on the practice range, and that I am watching as you take each step. It is with that thought in mind that I have prepared each chapter.

* * *

Anyone can play good golf, if he wants to. Now—it's up to you.

JOHNNY REVOLTA

CONTENTS

CONTENTS

ILLUSTRATIONS

SCORE CARD 1

Before reading this book, mark down the score of your last golf game. From time to time in your course of lessons you will be referred to other score cards on the end leaves to keep a record of your progress.

Hole	Yards	Par	Your Score
1			
2			
3			
4			
5			
6			
7			
8			
9			
10			
11			
12			
13			
14			
15			
16			
17			
18			

Total:

Name of Course:

Date:

1 | GOLF ISN'T SO TOUGH

SOME YEARS AGO a young woman came to me and said, "I'd like to take twenty lessons from you."

"I'm sorry," I replied. "I don't know that much golf."

Today, after more than twenty years of professional golfing experience . . . after winning some forty tournaments . . . after I have given over 13,000 golf lessons . . . I would still give that same answer:

"I don't know that much golf."

Golf just isn't that complicated.

Good golf is simple; and simple golf is good golf. It involves learning and practicing a few basic fundamentals. Not a mysterious set of actions by your wrists, feet, body, arms—as some golf writers would have you believe—but a few simple ideas.

I call them my short cuts to better golf.

Playing golf is like driving a car. Actually you perform many separate moves. You turn on the ignition. You step on the starter. You release the brake. You push in the clutch. You shift gears. You step on the gas. You let out the clutch. And the car is moving.

But how many times have you thought of all those things? If you did, the car would jerk and skitter around and you would probably run off the road. Instead, you drive instinctively. You *know*—without thinking about it—how to put a car in motion. Your feet and hands are trained to do the right thing.

1

The same should be true of golf. If you are worrying about all the separate moves in a golf swing, you are going to run off the road, golf fashion, and end up in the rough.

Look at the sketch by artist Jerry Gibbons.

It shows the typical duffer worrying about the little things in golf. I'm going to call this golfer "Danny the Duffer." You will meet him again in this book—just as you see golfers like him on every course. Golfers like Danny are confused by all the details someone has given them. I have found that most golf faults can be traced directly to these worries.

Don't be a Danny the Duffer.

The next time you find yourself worrying about your hands, feet, pivot, weight shifts, and other incidentals, remember Danny. You can see the trouble he is getting himself into. If you want to avoid his mistakes, relax. Think, not of many things, but only of two: hitting the ball and hitting it where you want it to go. That's all that counts.

In this book—as in my private instruction—I am going to teach you step-by-step, this system of getting results in golf.

We're going to start from the very beginning. The best way to cure golfing faults is not to make errors in the first place. One hour spent learning a thing right will save you days of trying to correct a fault. If you have golfing problems, you can begin getting rid of them right now—by turning the page, and studying your first golf lesson.

2 THE REVOLTA SYSTEM

GENE KESSLER, sports editor of the Chicago *Sun-Times,* recently asked me my system for teaching golf.

"Everyone must groove his swing to fit his physique," I replied.

That, in a nutshell, is my system. I don't have a tailor-made golf game to fit every golfer. Neither does anyone else. No two golfers are exactly alike. Some are heavy set, others thin; some tall and some short; some husky, others not. Obviously their golf games can't all be alike.

Yet many golfers try to copy the upright swing of the top-flight players. They are imitating men who started using that swing as youngsters and whose muscles were especially developed for that particular swing.

The average week-end golfer, whose muscles are set for life, simply can't copy that swing. But still some golf books would have you try. Too often it results in a cramped, unnatural, and uncomfortable game with poor scores that never improve.

I believe your golf swing ought to be manufactured especially for you. In this series of lessons, I'm going to help you construct your own golf game, a swing best suited to your own individual limitations.

It is based on four simple ideas—the proper grip, the right stance, the Revolta formula, and the quickie rhythm. In my years

4

of teaching, I have found it the easiest, fastest, and best system for learning good golf.

You will find my system differs from many others in another way. Most golf books start with the driver, then go down through the irons and a chapter on putting is tossed in. That's placing the cart before the horse. The system ought to be just turned around. Here's why.

The putter is the key club in better scoring, particularly for the beginner. Ability to sink putts is the quickest way to break 100. It is the only way to shoot par or subpar golf. In addition, the putter is likely to be the busiest club in your bag.

Most golfers will use their driver only fourteen times in a round of golf. On the other hand, they will use their putter anywhere from eighteen to thirty-six times, if they shoot par golf— more times, ordinarily, than any other single club.

So I start my students with that club.

From there I have them take up the short irons. They are the easiest to master because their lighter weight and shorter shafts make them easier to handle. Next, the longer irons. And finally the driver and other woods, the most difficult clubs to use properly. The longer shaft means that the swing travels over a greater area. More room for error.

The swing, hand action, and other features of the entire set of clubs are similar. But I believe it best to gradually work up from the easiest to the hardest clubs. You'll be learning to drive from the moment we take up the short irons. But, this way, you'll learn quicker. And better.

When someone comes to me for a golf lesson, I take him to the practice tee to hit a few balls. I just stand to one side and watch. I notice these points: How is he gripping the club? How is he standing? How is he swinging? Where is the ball going and why? I watch him take three putts; one from three feet, one from ten, and another twenty feet from the cup. I notice the same things: grip, stance, swing, where the ball goes and why.

I can tell what he does right—and what he does wrong.

As you progress through this series of lessons, I want you to do the same thing. You must become your own golf instructor and critic. You must learn to pick out your own golf game, your faults and their correction.

5

On each point of the game I will explain the principles involved, and the various systems of handling them. I will teach you the "feel" of the proper shot and the way I consider best to handle it. But the final decision must be yours. You must manufacture your own grooved swing and select the best way for you to play each shot. It is the only sound way to learn good golf.

I often hang around the practice tee before a tournament and watch the other professionals swing. Each of them does something different. I can imitate every well-known golfing star. If I wanted, I could change my own game and grip and swing exactly as they do. But aping other players wouldn't be right for my game.

For that reason, let me caution you against picking out a particular golf hero and then striving to imitate his every move. I have no idea of turning you—or any of my students—into a carbon-copy of Johnny Revolta. Instead, I look for strong points in my student's game; the things which I can help him do better. And I am looking for the faults in his game, the things I can correct.

Above all, I am trying to impart to the student the *feel* of good golf. I am trying to teach him to know, instinctively, when he hits the ball properly. And then to be able to translate that feeling into his own individual golf swing.

First, let's take a look at you. Your age, build, physical characteristics, and sex will all be important in evaluating your game. If you are a youngster, probably you can hit the ball a country mile but are erratic. Odds are that you slice—hit the ball so that it curves to the right.

You will do well to stop, look, and listen. You have a long time to play the game; it will pay you to take a lot of time on fundamentals to learn your golf right. It will also help to remember that golf is not a game of strength. It isn't who hits the ball farthest, but who sinks it in the fewest strokes.

Tommy Armour, the stylish, slender Scot, once took a heavyweight champion out to the golf course. The fighter, using the swing which had laid his opponents on the canvas, sent the golf ball flying in all directions at weird angles. Sometimes it would roll only a few yards. Sometimes it didn't move at all.

Armour meanwhile was knocking them out 200 and 250 yards.

"If you can knock them that far," argued the champ, "I oughta be able to hit the end of the clubhouse from here. There must be a trick to it."

He was right. There is a trick to it. Timing, form, and other factors that you are about to learn get yardage in driving. But the important thing, as the champ finally realized, is that mere strength isn't a substitute.

If you are a woman, chances are you will never hit a golf ball as far as a good man golfer. But you can add distance to your drives. Don't feel that because you are a woman you are limited to hundred-yard drives. You can—and will—hit them farther. And you have one big advantage in the game. Because most women are good dancers, they have a natural grace and sense of balance that makes a good golf swing come easier to them than to most men. They also avoid one glaring masculine fault: trying to "kill" the ball. We will have more to say to women golfers a little later on in this book, but for now a good word on which to start learning golf is this: Don't try to match a man's drive yard-for-yard. But you can, and will, learn other ways—particularly in the short game —to keep up with masculine company on the fairways.

If you are tall and lanky—whether man or woman—you have great potentialities. Having a long reach and ability to use longer clubs, you should be able to outdrive your shorter companions. But since your swing goes over a greater distance, you will have to pay particular attention to fundamentals to keep your swing under control.

The short and stocky player is likely to have waistline trouble. He may have poor balance and improper footwork. Many heavy-set golfers play entirely with their arms without turning for their pivot. Others stand flat-footed when they swing. This robs them of distance and accuracy. If you are on the heavy side, pay particular attention to the lessons on swinging a golf club.

The short player must also be very particular about his clubs. Too many have the fault of picking out long clubs in an effort to make up for their lack of height. If you are below average height, be especially sure that your clubs are right for you.

If you are past middle age, your greatest advantage in the game should be consistency. Most older golfers seldom vary more than a stroke or two. When I go out with one of them and allow him his handicap, I've got to shoot my best golf to win. If you are

7

in this group, you can add some distance to your shots, but most of your improvement must come through increased accuracy.

Some golfers are quite handicapped physically. One of the better professionals has a crippled arm, so thin you could circle it with your thumb and forefinger. Another has a trick leg from a football injury and it sometimes crumbles under him. Many golfers have but one arm or one leg.

I know one golfer who has heart trouble and can barely walk. Still he continues to play golf by means of an ingenious wheel chair that runs on a gasoline motor and carries him from shot to shot. I even know of some blind golfers who play creditable golf.

Physical handicaps are not a bar to golf—nor, even, to playing excellent golf. If you are handicapped, study carefully the fundamental points of the game: grip, stance, and swing. Then analyze the way your handicap affects these fundamentals and vary them to fit your needs. Actually, however, few handicaps require changing from the normal system of play. Only when you find that your handicap makes it absolutely impossible should you think about changing.

One final word. If some phase of your game is satisfactory now, just skip the chapter in the book covering that phase. If, for example, you now putt consistently, turn past that chapter in this book. If you are satisfied with your drives, why change? Experimenting will only confuse and wreck your game.

And now to the business of improving your score.

3 SELECTING YOUR CLUBS

CHOOSING THE RIGHT CLUBS will not necessarily make you a good golfer, but they are an essential. Poorly suited clubs will make you a poor player. You wouldn't buy a suit of clothes that didn't fit; don't make the error of buying clubs that don't fit.

There are three essentials to your clubs. They should be the right length, be the right weight, and have the right flexibility.

Getting the proper length in your clubs is most important in developing a sound, natural swing. Clubs that are too long or too short will force you to take an unnatural stance and swing.

As a general rule the attached chart, prepared by the Wilson Sporting Goods Company, will show the proper length clubs for most players:

MEN

Club	Under 5½ feet (inches)	5½–6 feet (inches)	Over 6 feet (inches)
No. 1 wood (driver)	42	42½–43	43½
No. 2 wood (brassie)	42	42½–43	43½
No. 3 wood (spoon)	41	41½–42	42½
No. 4 wood (spoon)	40½	41 –41½	42
No. 2 iron	38	38½	39
No. 3 iron	37½	38	38½

Club	Under 5½ feet (inches)	5½–6 feet (inches)	Over 6 feet (inches)
No. 4 iron	37	37½	38
No. 5 iron	36½	37	37½
No. 6 iron	36	36½	37
No. 7 iron	35½	36	36½
No. 8 iron	35	35½	36
No. 9 iron	34½	35	35½
putter	34	34½	35
sand iron	34½	35	35½

WOMEN

Club	5–5¼ feet (inches)	5¼–6 feet (inches)	Tall, Experts (inches)
No. 1 wood (driver)	41½	42	42½
No. 2 wood (brassie)	41½	42	42½
No. 3 wood (spoon)	41	41½	42
No. 4 wood (spoon)	40½	41	41½
No. 2 iron	37	37½	38
No. 3 iron	36½	37	37½
No. 4 iron	36	36½	37
No. 5 iron	35½	36	36½
No. 6 iron	35	35½	36
No. 7 iron	34½	35	35½
No. 8 iron	34	34½	35
No. 9 iron	34	34½	34½
putter	33½	33½	34
sand iron	34	34	34½

The average man should swing a club of normal weight—13½ ounces—the average woman, a 12¾-ounce club.

The average golfer likewise ought to use clubs with an average amount of flexibility. Since most clubs sold have a medium of "give" in the shafts, you are not likely to make an error in this regard.

There is, however, one error that some golfers make in choosing their clubs. They have read, or noticed, that nearly all professionals and good amateurs use stiff-shafted clubs. So they want to use them too, thinking there is some magic in the clubs.

Unless you shoot better than 80, you definitely should not use stiff-shafted clubs.

There is one exception. If you are a big, powerful golfer with a very fast swing and are a long hitter, you could use stiff-shafted clubs. By a long hitter I mean one who hits a ball 250 yards. Let's not kid ourselves on that distance. I mean *actually* 250 yards.

A golfer with a short, fast swing should use a club with a slight amount of flexibility. This type of golfer never takes his club back so far that the head dips below the horizontal. He depends on speed with his swing. I shoot that way. So does Lighthorse Harry Cooper, George Duncan, Chuck Ward of England, Sammy Berardi of the famous Old Elm Club in Chicago. Jimmy Demaret has a fairly fast swing. So do many others.

The golfer who takes a fuller swing so that his club shaft dips below the horizontal has a slightly slower tempo and a shade more time in his swing. He can use a shaft with a little more give to it.

The reason for varying flexibility in shafts lies in the fact that they bend during the swing and straighten out before they strike the ball. This straightening motion adds power to your swing. But the shaft must straighten out before you hit the ball or your shot will be distorted. The faster your swing the less flexible your shaft should be. A fast swinger with a "whippy" shaft will always be hitting with his hands ahead of the club head too far and his shots will go wild.

A whippy shaft should be used only by very portly gentlemen whose stomach prevents them from taking any more than a half swing, or by golfers with a very slow swing.

Women should use clubs with slightly more whip to them than a man's. The reason: they normally swing slightly slower than a man and the give in the shaft helps them gain distance.

In selecting your clubs let me strongly urge that you get a set made by a nationally known manufacturer. Sometimes golfers are tempted to buy a cheap set, particularly to get started with. But the initial savings, if any, will be small; and over the long run, you'll be money ahead by getting good clubs.

By all means get a matched set. By this I mean pick all your clubs from the same model by the same manufacturer. Each club in the set will be balanced with the others. A mixed up set will only give you trouble in standardizing your swing.

If you can't afford a full set right off, start with a few essential clubs and gradually add to your set.

The key woods are the driver and No. 3 wood.

The minimum irons are the No. 3, 5, 7, and 9 and the putter; or the No. 2, 4, 6, and 8 irons and putter.

As you add clubs, add them backward in number. Add a sand iron first. Then the No. 8 or 9 iron. Then the No. 7 or 6 iron, depending on which one you have now. And so forth until you have the full set.

With the woods, add the No. 4 or 5 wood first; then the No. 2 (brassie).

The reason for adding to your clubs in inverse order is that the shade of difference in clubs is most important in the short irons.

There are, of course, advantages to starting with a full set. It will insure a more evenly balanced game, since you will have all the clubs needed for a full game. But, if you live near a club where caddies are scarce, or if you prefer to carry your own clubs, remember that a full set can add up to quite a load. Don't overburden yourself with so much weight that you become uncomfortable.

There are a number of putters on the market. The most popular model is the gooseneck putter. But, the most important thing is to find the model that suits you best. The putter does not necessarily have to match your other clubs. Some golfers get excellent results with the mallet-headed club, like a croquet mallet turned sideways. But avoid the freaks; they are outlawed and generally are unsuited.

The clubs should feel right to you. The best club to test is the driver. If it feels right to you, so will the rest of the clubs in that set. If possible, take the set out to the practice tee and try them out. That's the best test to determine that you've selected wisely.

You will also find it smart to buy your clubs through a competent professional. Golf is his business and he is an authority on the game. A set of golf clubs is an important investment. A good pro will help you get your money's worth by assisting you in selecting the right clubs. I'm not trying to drum up business for the boys with that advice. It is just that I have seen too many golfers with poorly selected clubs that have unduly hampered their game and I know good professional instructors will take time to help you find the right clubs for your game.

A good pro can tell you—by watching you take a few practice putts and hitting a few long shots—whether the clubs you have picked out are right for you. Again let me repeat. Good clubs won't necessarily make you a good golfer; but they will keep you from being a bad one.

You will also find a pair of spiked shoes a good investment. They help you get a good solid grip with your feet, especially in poor lies and on wet turf. A good foundation is vital to a good swing.

Whether you wear gloves while playing is up to you. Few pros use them, but then, with their constant playing, their hands get well toughened up. I don't think gloves help or hinder your game. So that decision is strictly up to you.

Your clothing on the golf course is also a personal matter. The only important "don't," however, is not to wear clothing that is too tight. A golf swing depends on free movement of the body, so consider that point in choosing your golf outfit.

On sunny days, a golf hat is usually advisable. Sun glasses are likely to be a distraction and, for many golfers, to distort their judgment of distance.

But, above all, be comfortable. That's essential to relaxation so you can devote your thinking solely to the game. You will have to do that if you want to join the experts.

In closing this chapter, let me give you a few tips on caring for your clubs. When you put your set away for the winter, store them in a place that is neither too hot nor too damp. Otherwise the wood may crack.

If possible, hang up your bag of clubs. If they are leaned against a wall, for example, the weight may bend the shafts.

In caring for your woods, rub some linseed or machine oil into the club face, especially along the grooves. And drop some on the bottom along the crack formed by the metal plate. A little furniture polish will keep the rest of the wooden club head looking nice.

On your irons the best thing to use is soap and water. From time to time the face will get matted with dirt and grass. Simple washing is best. Be especially careful *not* to use sandpaper or emery

1 3

cloth on chrome-plated irons. If your clubs are not stamped stainless steel, the abrasives will wear away the chrome and your clubs will rust.

One final word. With the tremendous growth of golf since the war, facilities are available in most places for refinishing your woods. For a small amount, you can have those favorite woods sanded down and refinished with their factory luster. Good clubs deserve good treatment, so care for your equipment.

4 SECRETS OF BETTER PUTTING

THE AVERAGE GOLFER has two putting faults. He putts too short, or he putts the ball off to one side of the cup. Both are caused by an uncertainty about putting. Either the golfer has no "feel" for the proper putt, or he makes some mechanical error in his hitting so the ball doesn't go where he wants it to.

Danny the Duffer usually strides up to the ball, takes a quick look at the cup, grabs his putter, and slaps the ball in the general direction of the hole. He relies heavily on luck, hoping that the ball will somehow drop in. But it seldom does.

Or, maybe Danny has read somewhere that putting is, after all, an individual problem and that all you can do is keep trying. Or perhaps he has seen a picture of Bobby Jones or some other great putter and he says, "Aha, that's for me," and he bends himself into what he believes is this golfer's putting style and bangs away at the ball.

Danny is, as usual, only half right. Putting is an individual problem. There have been great putters with different styles. Some stand upright, some bend slightly, others crouch down over the ball. Some putt with their feet together; others with feet wide apart. Some putt with the ball off their left foot; others with the ball midway beween their two feet; still others off their right foot.

Just which putting style you use is up to you. Comfort and the results you obtain are the important matters in deciding your own style. But follow the basic rules for good putting. For, regardless of the differences in their general appearance, all great putters are following the same basic rules.

A putt is best described as rolling a golf ball to the cup. A well-executed putt never leaves the grass, but rolls along true for the hole. There are three factors in a good putt: (1) the angle of the putter; (2) the line to the cup; (3) the distance to the hole, or, stated another way, how hard you putt the ball.

For the moment, let us consider putting on a perfectly flat green. There is a straight line from your ball to the hole. It is obvious that your putter must strike the ball squarely in order to make it roll along that path. If the putter is slightly turned one way or the other it will send the ball off that straight line. It is also obvious that the putter must be traveling along the straight line to the hole when it strikes the ball or the blade will hit the ball a glancing blow and spin it off line.

Whatever your putting style, you have to meet those two requirements if you are going to putt well.

Let's start with the grip—how you hold the putter. It will be slightly different from the grip used on other clubs. We want the hands to closely balance one another. And we require less wrist action in putting than in other strokes.

There are a number of putting grips used to accomplish this balance. Most of them involve overlapping one or more of the fingers. The one I favor, and which is used by most professionals, might be called a "reverse-overlap." It was this grip that led Tommy Armour to say, "I've seen some nifty putters in my day, but this fellow has 'em all stopped."

To form this grip, study the step-by-step sketches together with the explanations.

There is another feature of the grip that must be explained: the tightness of it.

Grasp the club as tightly as you can. Notice how the muscles in your forearms tighten up? Obviously that grip is too tight. It would cause tension and your movements would be jerky. Now, loosen your grip so the club is almost ready to fall out of your grasp. This grip is obviously too loose; in striking the ball, the club would slip in your hands.

The proper grip is somewhat in between: just enough grip to keep the club from slipping in your hands.

Place your putter on the ground. Now, pick it up.

That's about the amount of pressure needed to grip the club. You didn't grab it with a strangle hold; nor so loosely that it fell from your grip.

Practice the putting grip. As you walk onto the green, take your proper grip. Check it over before you step up to the ball.

Now for the actual putting. Here you are aiming for a stroke that always travels in the same groove. You want to develop a grooved swing. If you always hit the ball the same way, it will always follow the same path. That's half the battle won in better putting.

Remember the swings you used when you were a kid—a rope thrown over a tree limb and a board or auto tire for a seat? Or the fancier ones in the schoolyard that had the metal supports? For your putting swing you also want a firm base. In this case, it will be your entire body, with the exception of your arms and hands. They alone will do the swinging.

Your body is going to form the base on which your arms swing the putter. You want them firm. So, once you have taken your proper stance, your body—feet, head, knees, torso—should not move. Again, as in the grip, I do not mean that you should stand rigid, nor that you should stand loosely, but somewhat in between. All that is needed is enough firmness so that your body forms an anchor on which your arms can move in the putting stroke.

As for your actual stance, the important thing is comfort. There are a dozen and one ways to stand in putting. Just pick out the one that you like best. But a few basic rules must be followed. The shoulders and hips must be parallel to the line the ball will travel to the hole. And, like a rifleman sighting down the barrel of his gun, the golfer must look down his putter at the ball as he prepares to hit it. This means he must be bent over at the waist. Most good golfers stand so that their head is directly over the ball.

As you noticed in the putting sketches, your knees should be bent. Here's why. Place your putter, its blade flat on the green, about six inches in front of your feet. Keep your knees straight. Now swing the putter back and forth with your wrists stiff. Feels uncomfortable, doesn't it? Your swing is erratic. To correct that

17

PUTTING

Sketch *A* shows the left hand grasping the putter. The thumb lies down the shaft, which is gripped by the last three fingers of the hand. The left forefinger is extended. In sketch *B* the right hand fits snugly against the left, the left forefinger falling naturally over the back of the right little finger, or ring finger, whichever is more comfortable.

The right hand may grasp the putter so the thumb points straight down the shaft. In this case the backs of both hands will be parallel to the shaft. I find it helpful, however, to crook the right thumb so the nail grips the shaft. This opens my right hand slightly. In either grip the back of the left hand faces squarely to the cup as shown in the bottom sketch *C.*

The dotted line represents the path to the cup. Notice that the face of the putter is at right angles to the line, the shaft is straight.

The center sketch shows my putting stance. Its exact details are unimportant. The important details are these: the knees are bent so the golfer is "sitting down" to the ball. The head is over the ball. The elbows are in close to the body. The shoulders and hips are parallel to the line of roll to the cup. In this sketch, I am lining up my putt.

In the two smaller sketches, I am actually putting. Note that nothing has moved except the arms swinging *from* the shoulders. The head has remained stationary. The putter is swung back, then swung forward to strike the ball. The sketches also show the proper sequence of putting. First, get the right grip. Second, line up the ball and get your proper stance. Third, swing the putter back and drop the ball in the cup.

you have to bend your knees. And bend the arms at the elbow and at the wrists. Keep your elbows in, not against your body, but close to it.

Study again the sketch of my putting position. Check the wrists, elbows, and knees.

You will notice that the more you bend your arms at the elbow, the more you must bend your knees to keep the putter flat against the ground. Some golfers prefer just a slight bend; others go into a deep crouch. Again, comfort is the big thing. Comfort means relaxation, an important factor in good putting.

Some golfers find that getting down into a deep crouch, close to the ball, helps their aim. Others find a slight knee bend gives them a better swing. Find the one that suits you best.

Now for the correct movement in putting. Put your club aside for the moment and take your stance. Instead of gripping the putter, simply clasp your hands together. Now swing them back and forth in front of you. That's the motion used in putting. Just like a pendulum. Now pick up the putter again and do the same thing. Like a pendulum. Back and forth. Back and forth. Keep your elbows in. Back and forth. Back and forth. Keep your head and body still. Keep that putter swinging.

Note that as you keep the putter swinging, there is a slight play in your wrists. They aren't rigid, but give a little with the motion of the swing. You will also observe that the putter is moving in the same arc every time. That is a grooved swing. With repetition, you will perfect this grooved swing so that every time you putt, your club will always follow that same path. The path that leads it right to the cup.

All right. Let's take a quick review. The club is gripped with both hands pushed close together, both thumbs pointing down the shaft. Backs of the hands, thumbs and blade of the putter are all parallel. All are at right angles to the line the ball will travel to the cup.

The knees and elbows are bent, the elbows in near the body. The head is right over the ball. Shoulders and hips are parallel to the line to the cup. The arms are swung back and forth, and the rest of the body stays still.

I putt in a half crouch, so my arms are bent almost, but not quite, to a right angle. I place the ball about six inches in front of my left foot. My right foot is about a foot to the right and slightly ahead of my left on short putts. On longer putts I put my right foot farther to the right so my feet are about shoulder-width apart for the thirty-footers.

I also crook my right thumb so the thumbnail is pressed against the grip. I find this helps me get a little better grip.

My style simply seems best to me. As long as you follow the principles for proper stance and swing, the incidentals make little difference. Try the various foot positions. Try the different knee bends. Try playing the ball off your left foot, midway between, and then off your right foot. I find it gives *me* a better stroke and improved aim by playing the ball off my left foot. But decide for yourself. Take the form which gives *you* the best results—then stick to it.

Now let's putt some balls. For the moment don't worry where they go or how far. Just get the feel of swinging the putter. Remember the pendulum motion. Don't stop your swing as you contact the ball; keep it right on going to complete the pendulum swing.

The motion should be natural. The follow-through will be approximately the same distance that was covered by the backswing. Some players make the error of exaggerating their follow-through, taking, for example, a one-foot backswing and a three-foot follow-through. This *un*natural follow-through destroys the naturalness of the swing.

Remember your head is part of the firm base of your swing. It has to remain still.

Don't look up until you think the ball has stopped rolling. Looking up too soon will pull your club out of its grooved swing.

Keep the blade of the putter close to the ground in your swing. Keep it along the line the ball must travel to the cup. A straight line. This is especially true for short putts. On long putts, your swinging motion will carry the club slightly inside the line and upward from the ground. But on the long putts, as the club comes into the hitting area it moves low to the ground and along the line of roll.

Forget about the ball for a moment. Just swing the putter back and forth. Back and forth. Notice that you are not swinging it back slowly and returning it slowly. You have a nice, even

21

rhythm. Remember that now as you putt the ball. The slow, hesitating stroke not only will cause tension, but will leave you with only a guess as to how hard to hit the ball. And you can't drop them in by guesswork.

Now put a golf ball down on the ground. Take your putter back and hit it. Remember that rhythm. Remember to take the club through for the rest of its arc. Try another putt. See if you can keep the same rhythm you used in the previous putt. Try another. Same rhythm. Another. Same rhythm. Back and forth. Back and forth.

Pick a flat putting surface and putt a half dozen balls. The practice putting green or your living-room carpet will do. It is obvious that if you hit the balls with the putter blade square, your swing in the same groove, and with the same rhythm, all the balls will end up in the same spot.

Notice that if you take the putter back only a few inches, the ball will go a few feet; but if, with the same tempo, you take the club back farther, the ball will go farther. That's the answer to the problem of distance in putting. If you have a short putt, the club face goes back a short ways; for a long putt, you take it back farther. But always in the same groove, with the same rhythm.

Notice how far the ball went and how far back you took the club. If you will do this faithfully, you will learn just how far back to take the club to hit the ball a particular distance.

That's the *ABC* of putting: (*A*) the same groove for every putt; (*B*) the same rhythm; (*C*) a short swing for short putts, long swing for long putts, the amount of swing determined by the distance.

It takes a lot of practice to learn putting. I spend a quarter of my practice time on the putting green. When I was a kid, I had a job as a pro's assistant. I'd gobble down my lunch and run out to the ninth green which was right in front of the pro shop and I'd practice until I had to go back to work again.

I also learned a trick for practicing at home that I think may help you. First I got a block of wood, two inches wide and two feet long. I cut a golf ball in half and nailed it to the end of the block. (Or you could round off the front edge of the block, if you want to.)

Practice putting with this block, hitting the ball on the round edge of the block. It will help you to develop that grooved swing,

22

so necessary to good putting. If you strike the block unevenly, it will not travel in a straight line. If you hit it squarely, it will move straight ahead.

It will also help you to avoid two of the big errors I notice in most students. They grip the club too loosely and they take too long a stroke. Another frequent error is caused by the golfer picking the club up with his wrists as he takes it away from the ball. This results in taking the club outside the proper line the ball must travel to the cup. Both hands should take the club away and bring it back.

You can also practice putting on your living room carpet. But remember this. Most rugs are faster than putting greens and the ball will travel farther. So use this practice aid only in learning to groove your swing and checking that you hit the ball in a straight line. It will also help you in picking the correct line to the cup if you aim for a target—preferably something the diameter of the cup (four and a quarter inches). But don't use this living room practice as a check of distances; it will throw your game off.

The best practice, of course, is on the putting green. Start with one-foot putts; then two feet; three feet; then four feet. Learn to sink these consistently. Then gradually work back a few feet at a time until you are trying twenty-footers.

Thus far we have discussed how to putt on a flat surface.

But there is another factor in putting—the greens themselves. Most of them are not flat; they are running uphill, downhill; they are filled with slopes that go every which way. They have a grain, just like your rugs. If they are packed tight and clipped short, the ball will roll farther. If they are wet, the ball won't go so far.

As you walk onto the putting green, approach the ball from behind. Look along the line from the ball to the cup. What lies between? If the green is slanting slightly downward to the right, a straight putt would roll off that way. So you aim slightly to the left, to let the downward roll carry the ball into the cup. A sharper roll will require aiming even farther up the slope.

After you have sighted down the line to the hole, take your proper grip. Step around and place your putter down in front of the ball so that it is square to the line you have selected. Then take your stance. Finally, move your putter behind the ball and take your stroke.

There is a good reason for this step-by step process. First you look over the situation and make your decision. Placing your putter in front of the ball blocks the ball from your vision so it doesn't interfere with your planning. At this point you are concerned only with choosing the proper path for the ball to travel. With your putter you mark that line. Then you take your stance so that your feet and body are correctly placed in relation to that line. Taking your grip before you step up to the ball enables you to make sure that you have the proper grip—so you can then forget about it completely and concentrate on the other factors for good putting.

Now you have the right grip and the right stance for the groove you have chosen. Finally you move the putter blade in back of the ball, select the amount of backswing needed for the distance and then stroke the ball.

That recalls a four-ball match in which Toney Penna ran into trouble. He and Herman Barron were paired against Gene Sarazen and Ben Hogan in the quarter-finals. They were 5 down after the morning eighteen. In the locker room at noon someone mentioned that Penna had no chance. The conversation ended up with Toney betting $10 against $1000 that he would win.

As they started the afternoon round, Penna and Barron got "hot" with birdies and eagles. By the time they reached the seventh hole, they were only 1 down. Toney had a beautiful drive and second shot. His ball was lying just a few feet from the cup. His opponents had taken a 4, so the putt, if he sank it, would even up the match.

But he was using a putter that was hollowed out in back. He laid his putter in front of the ball and sighted. Then he started to move it in back of the ball to putt. The ball caught in the back of the putter and his motion tossed it back off the green. That cost him a stroke. A chip shot back to the green and another putt added his score up to 5. It cost him the hole and the match. And the thousand dollars.

There are other factors on the green to affect your putt. The green may slope downhill between your ball and the hole. In this case you will want to ease your tempo slightly, because the downhill slope will make the ball roll farther. If the line of putt is

24

uphill, you want to hit the ball more firmly because the ball won't go so far uphill as on a flat surface.

The grain is another item to be checked. Run your hand over your living room rug. Notice that it is smooth one way and your hand glides over it easily. The other way—against the grain—is rougher and harder to move your hand against. Putting greens are the same way. The grass grows in one direction and forms a grain. When you putt with the grain, the ball glides over; against the grain the ball is held back.

Years ago we used to be able to rub our putters against the green to check its grain, but now that's forbidden. With practice, however, you will see that the grass looks darker when you are looking against the grain; shinier with the grain.

In Florida they use Bermuda grass for their greens and it is very grainy. In the $10,000 Miami Biltmore tournament I made my greatest putt because of the grainy green. I had lost a stroke on the sixteenth and seventeenth holes and I needed a four on the par-5 last hole to win. If I didn't, I would go into a three-way tie with Dick Metz and Jimmy Thompson.

I got a good drive and my second shot carried me up near the green. I scuffed my third shot and instead of landing near the cup as I planned, it dropped about twenty-five feet away. I got mad at myself for messing up that shot and I decided that this was one putt I wasn't going to hit short.

I hit the ball hard—too hard, as a matter of fact. It should have gone a good four or five feet past the hole. Fortunately for me, however, I was putting against the grain, which was like going against a hair brush, and it slowed down the ball. It scooted across the green, hit the hole and dived in like a scared rabbit. I have never seen a ball disappear so fast.

What do you do when you can't decide just which way the green slants? In that case take the safe course. Putt straight for the hole. The slope—whichever way it goes—won't carry the ball far off line.

Aim for this goal: never to take more than two putts on a green. Aim to sink those long ones if you can. But figure your line and distance accurately so that if you miss your shot the ball will lie close to the hole. In my opinion, a man who is a good

25

putter never leaves his ball more than two feet from the hole on his first putt.

Practice especially those one-, two-, three-, and four-foot putts. Try to drop your first putt in that area and leave yourself an easy second putt.

To improve your putting, spend plenty of time on the practice green, especially before going out to start a round of golf. At home, work with the block of wood to improve your grooved swing. Check and recheck your grip. If you have trouble with it, there is a device invented by Frank Strazza that I have found helpful in instruction. Made of plastic, it straps on your putter and its grooves automatically place the hands in the proper grip.

Study the greens. Learn to "read" them: wet, dry, grainy, slopes, and roll. Remember your errors. Picking the right line to the cup comes only with experience—but you have to be attentive or you will go right on making the same mistakes over and over.

It is worth working on. For good putting makes a good golfer and poor putting makes the dub.

But don't get discouraged. Some days those putts drop consistently and other times you can't do anything right. I remember Paul Runyon and I were paired in the 1937 Atlanta Open. On a par-3 hole we both landed twenty feet out on our first shot. We were considered among the game's best putters, yet we both took four putts to sink our ball!

And then there was the opening round of the Land of Sky tournament at the Asheville, North Carolina, Country Club in 1939. On the 225-yard seventh hole I sliced my drive and it landed on the far side of a creek that bordered the hole on the right. Trees blocked my path to the green but I lofted a niblick shot that cleared them and the ball landed on the green about twenty feet from the cup.

I lined up my putt and stroked it. It was too hard and ran four feet past the cup. My second wandered to the left and down the slope, ending up still four feet from the hole. My third putt went three feet over the pin, up the slope. My fourth came down the slope, a yard past the cup. My fifth, hit cautiously, stopped three inches short. Finally, I dropped it in with my sixth putt. Six putts on a par-3 hole! They built a monument to mark the spot.

26

Interestingly enough, that series of blunders actually helped my game. I had been putting badly all that season, but after that terrible showing, I was determined to redeem myself. I wanted very much to win and wipe out that stigma. And I almost did. Ben Hogan and I ended up just one stroke behind the winner, Dick Metz.

Start early the habit of playing one stroke at a time. Forget the ones you miss. They are past history. If you worry about them, the chances are you will make more errors and your score will go up. If you putt three times on a green, mark the score down and forget about it. Just keep aiming at that goal: no more than two putts per green. You may drop in your first putt later on and cancel out the lost stroke.

Remember this. Nobody plays perfect golf. One time Herman Uebele took a student out on the Willow Brook Municipal Course at Indianapolis, Indiana. He wanted to show the pupil, in action, how to use the various clubs. He ended up with a 60, thirteen strokes under par.

But that's not the whole story. In the round he missed four putts of three feet. He could have scored a 56, but didn't. Even with that excellent round, he could have done better. Even with some superhuman golf shots, he still missed some of the easy ones.

So will you. Everybody does. Good golfers merely miss fewer shots than the duffer. So aim to miss as few as possible—especially on the putting green. Drop your first putt near the pin, and sink the second. And your score will take a nose dive.

After you have studied the chapter on putting and put in enough time on the putting green to satisfy yourself that you are dropping them in, go out for a round and fill in score card 2 on the front end leaves.

If you took more than 45 putts, you'll find it helpful to go back and reread the previous chapter. Forty putts is good; thirty-six is very good. Under thirty is excellent. Spend at least one-fourth of your practice time on the putting green. Judge for yourself by your score how much time you need to spend on putting.

5 THE PROPER GRIP FOR IRONS AND WOODS

CLAYTON HEAFNER was playing at Pinehurst and hit a poor spoon shot. He stared at the duffed shot for a moment, then turned to his gallery and remarked sadly, "I've been told never to go around breaking clubs. But—" He walked off the course and smashed the club against a tree trunk. "But," he said, resuming his conversation, "I never liked that club anyway."

And then there was the time in the Beaumont Open when he landed off in the rough. He hit the ball; the ball hit a tree and dropped back at his feet. He swung and hit the same tree. He hit the ball a third time, again it hit the tree and bounced back in front of him.

"Pick up my ball," he told his caddy disgustedly. "We're going in."

"No, no," cried a woman spectator who had "bought" him for $450 in the Calcutta pool. "Don't pick it up."

"All right," said Haefner agreeably. And he didn't pick it up either. He just walked back to the clubhouse without it.

There is no denying that a dubbed shot tries the temper of everyone. I can't offer you any advice on deciding whether to throw your clubs in the nearest water hazard or whether to smash them. The best I can do is to help you avoid the common causes for muffing shots that make you want to commit a little golf course mayhem.

Many golf faults can be traced directly to a poor grip on the club. At first thought, gripping a club ought to be simple. Yet, in my experience, it is the most difficult of all golf lessons to learn. And in the grip lies the answer to good—or bad—golf.

A professional can deliberately slice or hook a ball by simply changing the position of his hands on the club. Later in our lessons you will learn how to do it too. I mention it now only to stress how important it is that you grip the club right—or you will hook or slice, but not deliberately.

Because it is so important, spend plenty of time learning the proper grip. This is an exercise you can perform in your living room without knocking over lamps and end tables. A few minutes a day spent practicing your grip will cut strokes from your game when you go to the golf course.

Pin this note in your cap: If you are having trouble with your shots not going where you want them to, check your grip. Most times you'll find your trouble there.

How should you grip a golf club?

In the last chapter we discussed putting and putting grips. You will recall that the grip I recommended linked the two hands together with the left forefinger overlapping the right hand. We wanted a grip that balanced both hands and we wanted little wrist action.

Now, however, as we move off the putting green and take up the rest of the clubs in the bag, we get into shots in which hand action is an important factor. For that reason we will use a different grip for the woods and irons. One grip for putting, another for all other clubs.

Fundamentally there are four basic ways of gripping a club. Each has had its champions. Chick Evans won the National Open with a palm grip; Gene Sarazen with an interlocking grip with his thumb outside; Lloyd Mangrum won with an interlocking grip with thumb inside; and nearly all the rest have won with the overlapping grip.

The palm grip is simply what its name implies. The club is gripped with both hands, much the way a baseball player holds his bat. Both left and right hands hold the club with all four fingers and thumb, and there is no interlocking of fingers or any other connection between the hands. For some, it produces more

29

power than other grips, but it is difficult to control. For that reason few golfers use it today.

The interlocking grip gains its name from the fact that the little finger of the right hand interlocks with the forefinger of the left hand, joining the two hands together. In one form of this grip the left thumb lies along the shaft and under the right palm. This is the "thumb inside" form of the interlocking grip. Another version has the left thumb outside—lying along the back of the right hand.

For the thumb-inside version, grasp the club in your left hand, the "V" of thumb and forefinger pointing toward your right shoulder. The thumb lies along the shaft. The right hand is pushed up tight against the left, with the little finger of the right hand interlocked with the forefinger of the left hand. The thumb of the left hand lies in the heel of the right hand. The thumb-outside grip is formed the same way, except in the very first step. For this grip, grasp the club in the left hand with the thumb around the shaft, baseball-grip style. Then the right hand grasps the club, the left forefinger and right little finger interlocking. Now the left thumb lies outside the right hand.

Some golfers have found that this grip eases the pressure on the thumb and wrists. Its advocates believe that it tends to knit the two hands together and prevents one hand from overpowering the other. But for most, it has the failing of not controlling the club on the backswing.

One of the country's great golfers is Claude Harmon of the Winged Foot Club. He changed from the overlapping to the thumb-outside grip in 1942. He found that his left thumb, lying under the shaft at the top of the backswing, was locking his swing and causing tension. He got that thumb out of the way with his new grip and took the Augusta Masters.

Although it worked wonders for him, Claude doesn't advocate that grip for most golfers. Like all good teachers, he points out that a golfer's grip is a matter of preference and of effectiveness.

But the majority of golfers will find the overlapping grip the best. Nearly all professionals use this grip. I recommend its use because I have found it is the best suited for nearly all my students. I believe you will find it advisable to learn, and use, this grip first.

30

Only after you have found it unsuited to your game, change to another.

The overlapping grip essentially consists of grasping the club in both hands, with the right pressed up tight against the left, the little finger of the right hand resting on top of the forefinger of the left hand. (Note that the left forefinger and right little finger are just reversed from the positions in the putting grip.)

There are endless varieties of overlapping grips. They differ principally in the position of the right thumb on the shaft, the angle of the hands on the shaft, and whether the club is gripped by the fingers, fingers and palm, or simply with the palms of the hands. Each of these variations has been worked out by some pro to fit his own particular needs.

The grip I have found satisfactory to most students is one in which the club is gripped by the fingers of both hands.

Study the accompanying sketches and explanation carefully now before I continue the discussion of the overlapping grip.

You will find it helpful to check your grip before a full-length mirror. At first you may get the impression that your right and left hands are pretty far over on the right side of the grip. But when you check it in a mirror, you will notice that the "V's" are pointed to the right shoulder.

Pay particular attention to the sketches and refer to them often. Spend plenty of time practicing the grip. Let me again remind you. The wrong grip results in hooks and slices.

Be sure your left hand is far enough over on the shaft. Most golfers have the fault of grasping the club with the left hand too near the top of the shaft. The "V" is pointing at their chin instead of their right shoulder. The left hand is the guiding hand—to guide for straight shots if you grip properly; to guide for a slice if you don't.

The "V's" if pointing right mean Victory on the course.

Even the best golfers are constantly aware of their grip. Frank Stranahan, one of the country's leading amateurs, has taken more golf lessons from different pros than any golfer I know. I worked with him briefly some eight years ago. One of the changes I advocated was in his grip. I felt he was gripping too high on the club with his right hand, causing tension through the right side of his body.

31

PROPER GRIP AND STANCE

The outside sketches show how your hands look from eye level, when you grip the irons and woods. The shaft of the club lies diagonally across the middle of the left hand, as shown in the first sketch. It is across the first joint of the left forefinger and below the heel of the left palm.

In the upper right-hand sketch, the golfer has simply closed his hand over the shaft. From eye level with left arm extended, you can see two or three knuckles. If you see fewer, your hand is not quite far enough over; if you see all four knuckles you are gripping the club too much with the fingers and your hand is too far over on the shaft.

In the lower left sketch, the right hand has grasped the shaft firmly with thumb and three fingers. The hand fits up firmly against the left. The right little finger overlaps the left index finger. Note that the right hand is slightly under the shaft, giving you a relaxed feeling in your right elbow. Both "V's" of thumbs and forefingers point to the right shoulder.

The lower right-hand sketch shows a common beginner's error. The "V's" are pointing wrongly upward or toward the left shoulder. Invariably with this grip the left arm is not straight, but is bent at the elbow. Note the difference between the right and wrong grip. In the wrong grip you can see the fingers of the *left* hand. Properly, you see the fingers of the right hand. This wrong grip will result in a slice.

The center sketches show the proper stance for a short chip shot. Note how close you stand to the ball, because this is a shot, not of power, but of accuracy. Knees are bent, weight evenly distributed and back on the heels. Note also that the club and left arm fall in approximately a straight line.

His grip remained the same, however, until the winter of 1948. I had a talk with him before the Miami Open. "I've made that change you talked about," he said. "I feel better, swing freer, and have more power now."

It wasn't a big change, although all the pros noticed it. Frank had won tournaments before. But with his new grip he shot rounds of 66, 66, 68, and 70 to take one of the country's big tournaments against the best professional competition.

6 GETTING STARTED RIGHT

A GOLF SWING, simply stated, consists of swinging a golf club away from the ball and then back to strike the ball. The club head is in the same position at the start of the backswing and at the point of impact. The backswing takes the club away, the downswing brings it back to the same spot from which it started.

The club head moves away from the ball in a groove and comes back in that *same* groove to strike the ball. That's what we mean by a grooved swing.

Also—for all practical purposes—the position of your body at the time you start the swing and when you hit the ball at the bottom of the downswing are identical.

So, half the battle for a good golf swing is won if you start right.

This starting position we call stance.

There is nothing mysterious about stance. I know you have heard a lot of complicated ideas about it. Well, forget them. Most of these complications exist because some golf teachers try to build a set formula for every golfer. As a result, most beginners bend themselves into an unnatural pose trying to imitate someone's system.

There should be no ironclad formula for stance. There are a few basic rules to follow, the rest is up to you. In building your swing, take the position that is natural for you. And be comfortable. "Doin' what comes naturally" was not only a good song, but a good golf rule.

Here are the fundamentals. I'll give them to you quickly now, and then we'll go into details.

1. Your club head should always lie flat on the ground.

2. Stand with your weight equally on both feet.

3. Stand with your toes pointing slightly outward.

4. Stand with your weight back on your heels.

5. Bend your knees slightly—a sort of sitting-down position.

6. With the No. 7, 8, or 9 iron (we will start with them), stand with your heels about six inches apart. That's just a starter, we'll experiment around in later chapters until we find the most comfortable position for your feet. Stand with your left foot about an inch farther back from the line of flight (the line from the ball to the cup) than your right foot.

7. Place the ball on a line midway between your heels.

8. Stand with your left arm in a reasonably straight line with the club shaft, and bend forward at the waist so your hands are slightly away from your body.

Before we go into an explanation of the whys and wherefores, let's try the stance once.

Take the proper grip on the club with the left hand only. Place the club face behind the ball, the bottom of the club resting squarely on the ground. Now place your feet, left foot slightly farther back than the right, the ball midway between your feet. Your heels are about six inches apart, the weight evenly balanced between the two feet. Your knees should be bent and your weight back on your heels. Now complete your grip by grasping the club with your right hand.

All right. Now let's go over the stance slowly, point by point, to clear up any uncertainties. As they used to say in the Wild West when they carried a man to Boot Hill, let's go feet first. We'll build the stance from the ground up.

Balance is going to be our prime concern. Scientific tests have shown that when the average golfer swings in a drive the club head travels between ninety and a hundred miles an hour. That means you've got to be well set, firmly grounded.

If you've ever played hopscotch, you know it isn't easy to balance yourself on one foot. Nor is it easy to swing a golf club ninety miles an hour with your weight balanced on one foot. Like a sailor on a rolling deck, get your weight evenly balanced on both feet.

Remember that. Your weight should be evenly divided between your two feet. That's important because so many pupils have peculiar ideas about standing with their weight on one foot or the other for different shots. Just remember the old adage and stand on your own *two* feet.

You will also find it helpful to stand with your toes pointing slightly outward. The reason will become clear in the next chapter when you start swinging a club. Suffice it for now to say that it will help your freedom of movement during the swing.

There is another important point in balance. Most golfers— 80 per cent of my pupils—have their weight shifted forward on the balls of their feet. They are off balance and in danger of falling forward on their faces.

Your weight should be back on your heels.

Rock back on your heels so your toes are off the ground, then rock forward so they touch the ground. Feel that weight back on your heels. That's where it belongs. You can feel your weight in the back of your thighs and the calves of your legs.

For a while you will have to remind yourself of those two points, keeping your weight back on your heels and evenly divided between your two feet. It is easy to forget until you have practiced enough so that it becomes automatic.

Bending the knees slightly is especially important. The knees act as shock absorbers. If you jumped from a wall onto the ground and landed with your knees stiff, you would jar your entire body. If, on the other hand, your knees were slightly bent, they would absorb the shock.

That is one good reason for keeping your knees bent in taking your stance. Another is that the bent knees will help make your movements in the swing flow evenly.

The combination of bent knees and weight back on the heels gives you a position best described as sitting down. Your posterior protrudes.

How much you bend forward at the waist is up to you. Your back, however, should be reasonably straight from waist to shoulder. Some golfers (particularly the tall and lanky ones) stand fairly erect, while the short and stock players are more likely to bend over farther.

There are only two other essentials. One, which I mentioned earlier, is that the base of the club head must lie flat on the ground. In a later chapter we'll go into the mechanics of golf when we'll discuss the fact that this position gives the best hitting area for the club and enables it to perform the functions intended by the manufacturer.

The other is that the left arm should be reasonably straight. By "reasonably" straight, of course, I don't mean rigid and locked, but comfortably straight. The left arm is the guide arm to the swing and keeping it reasonably straight will help you to develop a grooved swing.

The left arm and the club shaft should also form a reasonably straight line. This again enables the club to perform its proper function—the loft (or slant) of the club face will strike the ball at the proper angle.

Your hands, therefore, will be ahead of the ball. As you look directly at the ball, your hands will be on the left of your line of vision. (See the drawing on page 63.)

Also, it is obvious that the more you bend forward at the waist the farther away from your body your hands will be. Thus, for someone who stands fairly upright to the ball, his hands will be quite close to his body. The golfer who bends over markedly will have his hands well away from his body.

The position of the feet (about six inches apart, left foot slightly back) as I explained covers the No. 7, 8, and 9 irons. The width of the stance and the relative position of the feet will vary with different clubs. But don't worry about that now. We'll take up the other positions as we discuss the other clubs.

There is another point about the stance that you have probably noticed. The right shoulder is lower than the left for the very natural reason that the right hand lies lower on the club shaft. I mention it only because some students have a tendency to thrust that shoulder forward, when actually it should merely take its natural position parallel with the feet.

Again, let me put in a word about your balance. Just a reminder that it is vital to the process of getting started right. And now, let's put that golf game in motion.

7 THE REVOLTA FORMULA

WHEN I HAVE a pupil out on the practice tee, I give his game a periodic checkup to be sure he has grasped the fundamentals. Now —before we put your game to motion—is a good time for you to stop and review the points we have covered thus far.

Pick up your No. 7, 8, or 9 iron and take your stance.

1. Is your grip right?
2. Are your feet placed properly?
3. Is your weight balanced correctly?
4. Are your knees bent?
5. Is the club head flat on the ground?

If you had any errors in this quiz, correct them now. Once you put your golf swing in action these errors will be magnified and they will result in serious golf mistakes.

Do not make the mistake of rushing past those five points. In teaching thousands of pupils, I have learned that I must constantly remind golfers of these fundamentals. Several times in each lesson —not just the first lesson, but every lesson—I have to point out one or more of these factors to the student.

As your own pro, you will have to be especially alert for errors in these basic points. To overlook them—or to assume too early that you have them down pat—is simply to invite trouble on the golf course.

So don't read another line until you are sure of the five **answers** to the quiz.

Once you have them firmly in mind, you can proceed with the Revolta formula, the simple way to learn error-proof golf with a natural swing.

The first point is that of timing.

If you can remember back to· the day when you first **hit a golf** ball—or, if you have recently observed a beginner on a driving range—one thing will stand out conspicuously. There was no hesitation in the swing. The club went back, and, bang, swung for the ball.

That is the timing you should strive for. You should swing the club back and immediately bring it down again.

In my experience, one of the biggest factors in creating golf faults is the slow, hesitating swing. It results in lost motion and a waste of your hitting power. It results in tension, a deadly enemy of good golf. It is likely to throw you off balance, and, in turn, take your club out of its proper path to the ball.

This quickie rhythm is the third in my set of four fundamentals for good golf. The first two were: (1) the right grip, and (2) the proper stance. The last two (the quickie rhythm and the straight wrist)—the Revolta formula—we will discuss in a moment. All four go hand-in-hand. They are the *true short cuts to better golf*.

Some other golf systems teach a slow backswing. But they also require that you learn about weight shifts, pivots, when to cock your wrists, when to uncock them, and a lot of other details. I have found that the quickie rhythm, combined with the other three fundamentals of my system, does away with all these other details. That means an easier, quicker, and more effective golf system.

What do I mean by "quickie" rhythm? How fast do I mean for you to swing the golf club?

I mean you should swing the club as rapidly as you can and still control it.

I don't expect that idea to be perfectly clear at this moment. As you progress through this lesson, you will have a better conception of the speed which you can attain.

For a starter we are going to practice very short swings. **For** these exercises we will use this rhythm: One, two, three, swing! Repeat that phrase with a decisive tempo: One, two, three, swing!

You should be able to repeat the phrase twice in five seconds. That's the quickie rhythm for the short swing.

All right. Let's put that tempo to work. I want you to take your stance with the No. 7, 8, or 9 iron. We are going to start our swing with nothing except the arms.

Swing the club back about two feet. Keep your wrists straight.

Now swing the club down just behind the ball. Again take it back about two feet and then return it to the starting position. Keep your wrists straight. Nothing moves except your arms and the club, all moving as one unit. Take the club back two feet and return it to the ball. I want you to do that three times. Rapidly.

One, two, three.

Then, on the fourth time, hit the ball. Like this. One, two, three, swing! Remember the quickie rhythm. One, two, three, swing! On the first three counts you simply bring the club face just behind the ball; the fourth time you swing and hit the ball.

Study the sketches on page 43 that illustrate the Revolta formula.

Keep your wrists straight. This is an essential of the exercise. Your arms, hands, and the club must all move together.

Practice this ten times.

1. One, two, three, swing!
2. One, two, three, swing!
3. One, two, three, swing!
4. One, two, three, swing!
5. One, two, three, swing!
6. One, two, three, swing!
7. One, two, three, swing!
8. One, two, three, swing!
9. One, two, three, swing!
10. One, two, three, swing!

Now put the club down and take a little rest. Notice the feel you had in your hands? A feel of hitting the ball. That is vital to good golf. Power and timing come through proper hand action. You've started the job of *teaching* your hands the feel for the right swing.

THE REVOLTA FORMULA

On the adjoining page is a demonstration of the Revolta formula. This is the one-two-three-SWING exercise, designed to train the hands for the proper control and power in the hitting area.

The three sets of small sketches show the "one," "two," "three" steps in the exercise. The bottom sketches show the "SWING!"

In the first sketch the club is swung away and returned to the ball. Count ONE. The second pair is TWO. The third pair, THREE. On the fourth count the club is swung to hit the ball and to follow through.

Note the firmness of the hands throughout the swing, the lack of movement. This exercise is to train the subconscious mind for the proper starting movement—swinging the club back with a turn of the shoulders, the arms and club moving at the same time.

Notice that the head does not move until the final sketch when it raises naturally to follow the flight of the ball. The one-two-three-SWING movement is one continuous motion with the club moving as rapidly as possible while your hands still maintain control.

Note in the bottom sketches that the wrists "give" very slightly for the proper hand action to put life and crispness into the swing.

The three large sketches are also accurate illustrations of a good chip shot. Disregard the smaller sketches when you study the chip shot in the next chapter and consider only the bottom three drawings. The club is swung away at the left, in the middle it strikes the ball, and on the right it is following through. Note that the follow-through is approximately the length of the backswing.

43

Notice too the shock-absorber action of your knees. They give slightly with the power of the swing. That's why, in teaching you the stance, I told you to stand with your knees bent.

Relax for about five minutes.

Then do the straight-wrist exercise ten more times. Remember, the arms, hands, and club move as a single unit. Keep that same steady rhythm, moving the club as rapidly as you can. One, two, three, SWING!

After the tenth time, stop and take another breather. Now, do you notice something else about your swing? On the first three counts you kept your wrists straight. But on the SWING did you notice a little give in the wrists? You loosened them a little as you swung to hit the ball. Not much, just a little loosening of the wrists. That's part of the process of educating your hands.

I want you to *think* in terms of holding your wrists straight. That necessary slight looseness in the wrists will come naturally as you swing for the ball *without your thinking about it.* I mention it only to keep you from getting misconceptions about that movement. Just keep thinking of holding your wrists straight, that slight looseness will occur *unconsciously* in the natural process of swinging.

Notice something else. Notice what happens to your shoulders as you swing. They pivot. Not only your arms, hands, and club are moving together—but your shoulders are also turning as part of that unit.

After a short rest, do the exercise another ten times. Don't take the club back any farther than about three feet. But as you are swinging, notice that new awareness in your hands— an awareness of their function in swinging the club. Notice how the shoulders turn, the shoulders, arms, hands, and club all in one unit.

Notice, too, how far that ball is traveling even though you are swinging only a few feet. The reason: there is power, there is coordination, there is timing in that swing.

Keep practicing until the movement of shoulders, arms, hands, and club are totally familiar to you. It is an exercise you can do at home—simply taking your SWING without hitting a golf ball.

Now let me explain to you the reasons for this exercise. You have been learning a basic part of the Revolta formula. The area of your swing—two feet—is the core of your swing. With every

44

club, this is the hitting area. You are training your hands to have the right position as your club contacts the ball—arms, hands, and club in a straight line. You are also training your hands—and your mind—for the right feel in starting your swing.

That is only by way of explanation to impress upon you the importance of spending plenty of time on the exercise. And now, if you are properly impressed, forget the explanation. My purpose is not to teach you—but to teach your hands. And your hands can be taught only if you will repeat the straight-wrist exercise often enough so that you get the feel of the properly executed shot.

Once you have mastered this short stroke, lengthen your swing a little. Keep the same rhythm. Keep your wrists straight. One, two, three SWING! Move the club back about two feet, at first. Then gradually lengthen your swing. Nothing moves except your shoulders, arms, wrist, and club—all as one unit. Your knees, bent in the sitting-down position, take up the shock, giving a little with the natural motion of the swing.

When your swing has reached a point where your left hand is about even with your right hip, stop! That is as far back as I want you to swing the club for now. After that something else takes place in the formula, and we are not quite ready for it yet.

Spend plenty of time on this exercise. I recommend to my pupils that they practice it at least two hundred times. That sounds like a lot of practice. But it is time worth spending. And it will save you time in the long run.

It will teach you the feel of proper hand action in the hitting zone, a lesson that other golfers will take years to learn and many will never learn.

And—as you will find out in the next chapter—you have already learned most of the points involved in the chip shot, a key shot in reducing your score.

8 CHIPPING FOR THE CUP

WHEN SAM BYRD left the New York Yankees' outfield to become a big-time golfer, he came to me for lessons. "I always could bang the ball off the tee," he explained. "So when I decided to play golf for a living I figured it would pay me to take lessons from a guy who could show me something about using irons."

Ellsworth Vines came to me after he quit as an outstanding tennis star to become a professional golfer. He wanted to know my secrets for playing the short ones. Others of my prize pupils have been Patty Berg, Betty Hicks, and Alice O'Neill. And there have been plenty more. Even though they are now top-flight golfers in their own right, most of them stop around about once a year at my club to have me check up on their short game.

Today too many beginnners concentrate on trying to knock their drives a country mile. But the professionals know it is the short game that counts in making a good score. As I told you in the chapter on putting, when I was a kid I got a job as a pro's assistant. I had to keep an eye on the shop, and that meant I never could get more than sixty yards away for fear someone would steal something and I'd get fired.

Fortunately the ninth green was in that area. So all the practice I could get in was either in putting or in short iron shots. I didn't know it then but I was building one of the strongest parts of my game. When I stepped into the big tournaments for the first time in 1932, I was just a gangling youngster competing with the big stars of the day: Walter Hagen, Gene Sarazen, and the rest. But in my first attempt I came in second, only one stroke behind Denny Shute.

"John Revolta, youthful Menominee, Michigan, professional, laid a beautiful chip shot dead to the pin at the 54th hole for a 36-36 72 in today's morning round of the $10,000 Miami-Biltmore Open Golf tourney," one newspaper account read.

Later on, some reporters and professionals called me the "Iron Master." Some have even called me the greatest iron player on the links. I don't know about that, but I do know that dropping them into the cup from off the green can make you a good golfer.

As you have already discovered in an earlier lesson, it is easier to sink your putt from four feet than from thirty feet. Your putting task will, therefore, be increasingly easier as you get your shots from off the green in closer and closer to the pin.

How many times have you read that so-and-so won a particular tournament and one-putted a half dozen or more holes in a round? Take it from me that champ wasn't dropping in many 25- and 30-foot putts. More likely he was tapping them in from three and four feet away. Because he had dropped his previous shot in close to the pin.

You can too.

If you have learned the Revolta formula in the preceding chapter and have practiced it faithfully, you are well on your way. Because chipping is little more than using the formula on the golf course.

First of all, what is a chip shot? It is the shot used when the ball lies within ten feet of the green. The putting green, as you know, is surrounded by an apron or fringe of grass. You can't use a putter accurately from there, because the heavy grass slows the ball and either stops your shot or makes it erratic.

So you use a chip shot to stroke the ball onto the putting green.

Or, sometimes your ball will come to rest on the fairway at the base of the incline onto the putting green. Here again your problem is to stroke the ball up onto the putting surface. A chip shot is the answer.

Before we go into the details, let's get a clear picture of what we want to do with our chip shot. We want to knock the ball into the air. We want it to land just on the putting surface. And then we want it to roll to the cup.

There are three clubs used for chip shots: the No. 5, 6, and 7 irons.

Just which club you use will depend on the distance you want the ball to roll on the putting green. The shorter the roll, the greater the loft of the club chosen. The greater loft, or slant, to the club the more backspin the ball will get. So a shot with a No. 7 iron will roll less than a No. 6 shot; a No. 6 shot less than a No. 5.

Here is a good rule to follow: Use the club with the least possible loft. Thus, if you are only a foot off the putting green, use the No. 5 iron. The reason: you want the ball to fly low and roll as far as possible. It is easier to control on the ground than in the air. And, then too, a rolling ball can run into the cup even if it is hit a little too hard. A ball in the air, hit too hard, will simply land beyond the cup.

If, on the other hand, you are lying ten feet off the green and the pin is only five feet from the apron, you will want to hit the ball into the air to clear the intervening space, but you don't want the ball to roll a dozen feet past the pin. So you use a No. 7 iron to cut down the roll.

From the same position—ten feet from the green—but with the pin a dozen feet farther on instead of only a few feet, the No. 6 iron would be preferable. The reason: you can now follow the rule of using a club with the least loft. You want more roll than a No. 7 iron will give. From the same position—ten feet from the green—and with the pin now fifteen or twenty feet from the edge, you would use a No. 5 iron because you want the maximum roll.

With practice you will learn how far the ball will roll after you hit it with a No. 5, 6, or 7 iron. Consider the distance the ball must go in the air to reach the green. Obviously the greater the distance, the harder you will have to hit the ball and hence the farther it will roll. Then consider the distance the ball must roll to reach the cup—but not roll past it.

Always aim to drop the ball as close to the edge of the putting green as possible.

Let the amount of roll from the edge of the green to the cup determine which of the three chipping clubs you will use. And where you have an option, use the club with the least loft.

To make a chip shot, take a shorter hold on the club. Take your grip farther down on the shaft—somewhere in the middle of the leather grip is about right for most golfers. This gives you the maximum control of the club. Then simply use the Revolta formula. And presto! You have the chip shot.

Weight evenly divided, back on the heels. Feet for this shot can be even closer together than we discussed earlier. No more than six inches apart, and you can place them as close as two inches between the heels. Your left foot is slightly back of the right, with reference to the line from the ball to the cup.

Don't forget, in taking the shorter grip on the club, to get the proper grip. "V's" pointing to the right shoulder. Then, just take the club back and return it in the quickie rhythm of our exercise. The ball is played off the left foot. In the Revolta exercise you played the ball from midway in your stance. Actually this adjustment in the position of the ball is very slight because the feet are so close together.

As soon as you are confident that you have the formula down pat, you will want to eliminate the "one, two, three" preliminaries. So, simplify your motions to a backswing and downswing. To do this, use the words "one and two." One (swing the club back) and two (swing it down). One-and-two. But, remember the quickie rhythm. Aim for that quick, decisive tempo. Swing that club as quickly as you can, and still control it. There is the slightest pause on the "and" count of one-and-two; the faintest possible hesitation as your club changes direction.

As in putting, the amount of backswing will determine the distance the ball will travel in the chip shot. Notice, as you practice this shot, how little backswing is needed to send the ball a considerable distance. In your practice sessions, note carefully the distance the ball travels as you increase your backswing. Notice, too, the flight in the air and the roll from all three of your chipping irons. This will help your judgment of distance and selection of the right club as you encounter chipping problems on the golf course.

That's all there is to it.

But now—much as I dislike the usual "don'ts" in golf instruction—let me point out more common errors in chipping in case you run into difficulties in this phase of the game. If you don't, so much the better. Just skip over the next few pages to the next chapter. But if you are in trouble, pick out your problem and read the answer to curing it.

Topping the ball. There are two common causes for dubbing a chip shot. One is that the golfer tries to lift the ball onto the green. He fails to understand that the loft of the club will get the ball into the air, and he gets the idea in his mind that he has to help it along by scooping it into the air. As a result he lifts his club up as it reaches the ball and the bottom of the club hits the ball, sending it rolling instead of into the air. Moral: The club is built to get the ball into the air. Concentrate on hitting it right; the club will do the rest.

The other common cause for topping is an old bugaboo of beginners: looking up. The novice is usually a little uncertain about his game, and he wants to get a quick look to see what happened to the ball. The result is the same as the scooper motion mentioned above. In looking up the hands are pulled up, and with them the club, and again the bottom of the club head—instead of the hitting surface—contacts the ball. Moral: Once you've hit the ball, you can't change the shot. Like the porter in a girls' dormitory, don't peek. If in doubt, keep looking at the spot where the ball originally rested until you are sure it has stopped rolling. Better to wait and see the ball in the cup, than to sneak an earlier look and muff the shot.

Another common fault is a baby version of the hook or slice. Instead of going straight to the cup, *the ball flies off either to the right or left.* This is caused by not taking the hands back together and returning the club face squarely so that the wrists are straight when the club head meets the ball. If the ball flies off to the right, the left wrist has been late in returning at the moment of impact. If the ball flies off to the left, it is because the left wrist has collapsed and, in the hitting area, the right hand has turned over the left.

Moral: Practice the Revolta formula more. You haven't yet learned it thoroughly and you are letting your wrists go loose. Your hands must be firm and bring the club in straight to hit the ball squarely.

Hitting the ground in back of the ball. This is another possible error when you let your hands go loose, instead of hitting firmly and decisively. The left wrist has collapsed and the club slaps into the ground instead of hitting the ball. Moral: Like the previous fault the remedy lies in additional practice with the formula to teach your hands the right feel in the hitting area.

Dubbing the shot (the shot that falls short of its mark). This is usually caused by a failure to follow through. After the club head strikes the ball, it should keep right on going. Let the club stop itself by the natural slowing down process. Some beginners get the idea that they can put more backspin by hacking at the ball and stopping the club just as it contacts the ball. This just won't work.

Moral: The club face will put backspin on the ball. Swing the club as if it were passing right through the ball, the club will do the rest. Practice the swing—without a golf ball—until you get the feel of the follow-through, then put it to work with actual shots.

Another cause of the dubbed shot is hesitation. The golfer takes the club back the proper distance and starts his swing. As he does so, he suddenly thinks to himself, "Holy smokes, I'm going to hit it too far." He immediately clamps on the brakes. The result is to throw the club head out of line or to spoil the tempo. Moral: Decide before you take the club head back, how far you are going to take it and how fast you are going to swing. Then stick to your decision. The middle of a golf swing is no place to change your mind. With practice and experience, you can gain confidence in your ability to judge the stroke and distance.

There is one golfer at my club who looks like a champion on the driving range. His fairway game is excellent and he gets up near the green in expert fashion. Yet he has never broken 100 and probably never will until he learns to have confidence in his chipping game. He is never sure what he is going to do when he chips the ball and he blows up regularly within thirty yards of the cup. Moral: Learn your capabilities and then have confidence in them.

When Herman Keiser won the 1946 Masters tournament at Augusta with phenomenal work around the greens, Horton Smith gave reporters the reason. "He learned his golf at the short Glenstone course at Springfield, Missouri," Smith declared. "So he learned his chipping and putting first. Later he added the long shots to his game."

That's a good lesson for every golfer. The short shots are a vital part of the better golfer's game. Properly executed, they not

51

only knock strokes off your score but they also form a basis for correctly executing all the other shots. Work, and work hard, at chip shots. Combined with putting, they are the pay-off strokes of golf.

If you have the chip shot perfected, check your game on score card 3 on the front end leaves. If your score previously was around 120, you may take off as many as 10 strokes with a good chipping game. If your starting score was about 90, you should be able to improve your game by at least 2 strokes.

Where it says "your mark" on the score card, mark an "X" if you chipped to the hole and sank the ball either on your chip or with one putt. Mark a zero where you chipped and still needed two, or more, shots to sink the ball. Every zero means a lost stroke that you can, and should, pick up with practice on your short game.

9 HITTING THE SCORING ZONE

A PROFESSIONAL GOLFER with plenty of distance in his wood shots is likely to be on the green or close enough to use a chip shot. But the average golfer, without that added distance, normally will be using an approach shot on the third shot of a par-4 hole. It is a very demanding shot.

It means hitting the green from somewhere up to 100 yards out, and hitting it squarely. It means hitting it right so the ball lands and stays on the green without rolling off. It means hitting the green instead of going into the sand traps and other hazards around it. A pretty tough assignment.

For the average golfer the normal full shot with a No. 8 iron will carry 100 yards and the No. 7, 120 yards. Within the scoring zone, we will use a No. 7 iron or less—a No. 8, No. 9, sand iron, or pitching iron. A pitching iron is similar to a sand iron in design.

A little later on we will discuss fully the question of just which club to use and why. But for now we will take up the formula again.

As you recall in an earlier chapter we confined the swing to a short backswing, keeping the wrists straight. We turned this exercise into chip shots by taking a shorter grip on the club. Now, however, we will need more distance with the approach shots. That means a longer swing.

Let's gradually build up to the longer swing.

Take your stance with a No. 7, 8, or 9 iron with the regular grip about a half inch from the end of the shaft. Now go back over the formula as far as you have learned it so far. So back to the quickie rhythm: One, two, three, SWING!

Gradually extend the length of your backswing. On the counts of one, two, and three, bring the club down only as far as the ball; then on SWING hit the ball. Keep that club moving as fast as you can in quickie rhythm.

Your heels should be about six inches apart, knees bent, the left slightly farther back than your right, and your weight evenly balanced and back on your heels.

Starting with a backswing of about one foot, keep your wrists straight. Then increase the backswing to two feet. Still with your wrists straight. Then three feet. Still with your wrists straight.

Gradually lengthening your swing, take it back as far as you can, and still keep your wrists straight. Notice what is happening to your knees. They are giving more and more with the swing as it lengthens. The left knee is giving in toward your right leg on the backswing, then straightening on the downswing and your right knee is bending in toward your left leg on the follow-through.

You aren't *thinking* about bending your knees. It is just happening, that's all. The quickie rhythm and the straight-wrist exercise make it happen. Nothing very complicated about that, is there? Yet that is the process which other systems label "weight shifts" and make a lot of fuss about.

As you gradually lengthen your backswing for approach shots, you will notice something else. As you reach the limit of the swing in which you can keep your wrists straight (somewhere, ordinarily, around waist high) you will feel the weight of the club pulling your hands up.

When you reach this point, lengthen your backswing a little more and *let the club bend your wrists*. The motion of the swing causes your wrists to bend naturally. Simple? Of course. That in other systems is the complicated business of cocking your wrists.

In the natural motion of the downswing, you will find your wrists automatically uncock. Throughout the backswing and downswing keep your left arm reasonably straight.

Let me pause here and discuss the single most important point in good golf—*hand action*.

Hand action is what causes the whoosh to a swing. It is the zip, the pep, the power, the life of the swing.

Too many golfers confuse hand action and wrist action, and in their confusion doom themselves to the permanent status of duffers.

Your wrists bend naturally. That's part of the mechanics of the bodily functions. Simple as that fact is, duffers don't fully understand it.

Most beginners slice. An important reason for slicing is their habit of *picking up* the club at the start of the backswing. They take their stance and then bend their wrists back to start the club on the backswing. They are thinking in terms of wrist action.

This is true of most beginners and of most golfers who fail to break 90.

By contrast, what does a good golfer do?

The good golfer *swings* the club away, his shoulders turning in a spontaneous movement. The turning motion of the shoulders starts the backswing—the arms and club merely follow.

It is a spontaneous movement. With the proper quickie rhythm it happens quickly. Naturally.

As I have pointed out in the one-two-three-SWING exercise, the wrists are straight during the one-two-three part of the exercise. But on the SWING count there is a slight give in the wrists. That is *hand action*.

With very short chip shots there is practically no hand action. There is only the slightest give in the wrists. As your shots get progressively longer, there is more and more give in the wrists. As a result there is more and more hand action as the shots get longer.

If both my wrists were broken and taped up, I could still swing a golf club. But I would do it in mechanical fashion. There would be no whoosh in my swing. There would be no life. It would be like a driving machine.

Now, what is the difference between hand action and wrist action? Wrist action is the conscious cocking and uncocking of the wrists during a golf swing. Hand action, on the other hand, is the *controlled* action of the hands. It is somewhere between stiff, unyielding wrists and the other extreme, loose flopping wrists.

55

Learning hand action is one of the primary reasons behind my teaching you the one-two-three-SWING exercise. In the one-two-three part of the exercise I am deliberately teaching you to hold your wrists straight and firm. In swinging the club rapidly just to the ball, you force your wrists to remain firm and your hands to be in control of the club.

On the SWING count you have the freedom of the fuller swing—enough to produce that give in your wrists and yet to have complete control over the club. And that is hand action.

Again let me stress that hand action is the natural result of a good golf swing.

You don't have to worry about it. It will simply happen.

I have taken time out from this lesson to explain it principally to impress upon you that hand action will not occur if you consciously cock and uncock your wrists. It will not occur if you pick up the club at the start of the backswing by bending your wrists instead of swinging the club away.

With good hand action you will swing the club away for the backswing. And the downswing will have that satisfying whoosh of the club shaft that signifies power, control, and distance.

Try the one-two-three-SWING exercise again. First with a short backswing, then with a gradually longer backswing. Swing the club away. Return it. Swing the club away. Return it. Swing the club away. Return it. Swing the club away. SWING through the ball and on into your follow-through.

The important thing in the downswing is proper footwork. I often refer to the downswing as the automatic act of rebalancing. At the top of the backswing the body is coiled, the wrists are cocked, the left foot is turned over on its side and the left knee is bent inward toward the right.

In the process of the downswing we want to regain our starting position. The primary thing that happens is that the feet once again become firmly planted on the ground at the moment of impact. For that reason I lay great stress, in teaching, on proper footwork. If you have taken the proper natural backswing, your footwork will be perfectly timed with your swing. That perfect timing will then follow naturally as you rebalance yourself in the downswing.

There is one other factor to consider as you gradually lengthen your backswing in the one-two-three-SWING exercise. With the longer swing, your follow-through will be lengthened. Let that club fly on the follow-through, keeping your left arm straight as long as it is comfortable. It will be high—probably your hands will be about shoulder high. Then let your arms and wrists give slightly.

This natural swing will carry the club past the ball and on up. This motion, you will notice, will also pull your head up. Let your head follow this natural movement. There is no danger of looking up if you let this movement be natural. It is the unnatural looking up which ruins shots. And, interestingly enough, the unnatural position of staring too long at the spot where the ball was—resisting the natural motion which pulls your head up—will also ruin your shots.

In other words, let nature take its course—on both the backswing and the follow-through.

One final word on the backswing. As you approach the limit of your swing with your wrists bent, you will notice that your left knee not only bends in toward your right leg but, in the full swing, will cause your left foot to roll over on its side. Or, for some golfers, this natural motion will cause their left foot to go up on the toe. O.K. That's fine. That's what it is supposed to do.

Get the right grip. Get the proper stance. Start your swing with your wrists straight, shoulders pivoting your arms, hands, and club in one unit. Use the quickie rhythm. For the rest of the details let your body flow with the swing.

When you have the exercise well practiced with the one-two-three- SWING rhythm, change over to the regular swing. Swing it away—hit it! Don't bother with preliminaries. Just take the club back and swing for the ball. Still with the quickie rhythm. One-and-two. Swing it away—hit it!

Now, let me issue a warning on the basis of having taught thousands of golfers like yourself. Now is the time you are most likely to forget your earlier lessons. In concentrating on the swing, you are likely to let your grip go sloppy. You may forget your proper stance. Many students forget that sitting-down position of knees bent.

I have given you a simple system for learning the golf swing. But, because it is simple, it requires that you thoroughly learn all the fundamentals. So just because you learned them thoroughly once, don't take them as a matter of course. Keep checking.

Another note of warning. Don't try to hurry the learning process. As I have emphasized many times, I am teaching your hands the right feel for the proper swing. And I am trying to teach you to think only of hitting the ball. Only with practice can you get the confidence and experience necessary to convert these lessons into a good golf game.

Now we are ready to put the formula to work on the approach shot. In the last chapter we discussed the chip shot, and we learned that it is used in the area up to ten yards off the green. The clubs used were the No. 5, 6, and 7 irons.

As we move farther away from the green, we will require a shot that will carry to the green and roll to the cup—but not roll so far that it keeps right on going off the putting green. For this reason we will use clubs with more loft—more slant to the club face—which will give a backspin to the shot and hold the ball on the green.

The club to use for approach shots is the No. 7, 8, 9, sand iron, or pitching iron.

From ten to fifty yards off the green any of these five clubs can be used. Just which one you use depends on the problem confronting you. If there is a clear shot at the green—that is, if there are no sand traps or other hazards blocking the green directly in line from your ball to the cup—I prefer to use a No. 7 iron. This club produces a low-flying ball with plenty of backspin. I find that the lower flying ball is easier to control and gives me better aim at the cup.

If, on the other hand, the green is blocked by sand traps or other hazards, you have to aim for the green and give the ball plenty of stop. This dictates a club with more loft.

How much loft? Again, a safe rule to follow is that one we discussed in the chapter on chip shots. The closer the cup to the point where your ball must land, the higher-lofted club you must use to keep from overrunning the pin. For a medium run, the No. 8 iron is best. For a short run, the No. 9. And for a ball that will stop practically dead, a sand iron or a pitching iron is best.

A sand iron is a valuable club to have, if you do not already own one. We will discuss this club at more length in a later chapter on sand-trap shots. It is a club with a heavy sole (bottom of club head) that prevents it from digging into the sand or turf and its loft gives the ball plenty of backspin. Its weight—heavier than other clubs—encourages a natural swing.

Generally speaking, I believe it advisable in selecting your club for the approach shot to follow the rule I set out for chip shots: use the club with the least loft under the playing circumstances.

Like the chip shot, approach shots are played with the ball off the instep of the left foot. Likewise you will use the same slightly open stance (left foot about an inch or two farther back than the right). Since approach shots are longer than chip shots, you will have to take a longer swing. For this reason your feet will be slightly farther apart. Where most people play chip shots with their feet an inch or so apart, approach shots usually are played with the feet about six inches apart.

As you have discovered in the formula exercises, the exact distance is up to you. It is solely dictated by balance and comfort. In my teaching, however, I have learned to watch for one flaw. Most beginners spread their feet too far apart on short shots. With these close-in shots the power is very secondary to the accuracy put into the swing by the hands. So you don't have to get set for a home-run swing.

From very close in you may find it helpful to use the shortened grip on the clubs, just as you did with chip shots. But for medium- and long-approach shots use the full length of the club shaft.

For approach shots 50 to 100 yards to the green, use either a No. 8 or No. 9 iron. In most cases the No. 8 iron is proper. The exception—the No. 9 iron—is advisable only when the green is very small or when it is blocked by trees or other hazards that dictate an unusually high shot with a maximum of backspin.

For the average player the full distance with a sand or pitching iron is about 50 yards. A No. 9 iron shot will travel 90 yards and a No. 8 about 100 yards. A No. 7 iron shot will carry about 120 yards for the average player. Beyond that we are outside the scoring zone.

Approach shots require plenty of practice, experience, and confidence.

As in the chip shot, Danny the Duffer is unsure of himself and dubs the ball.

In approach shots use the formula rhythm—one-and-two. Hit the ball decisively and without hesitation. Use a short, definite swing in preference to a longer, slower shot. The reason: the short, decisive shot will produce a low-flying ball with plenty of backspin and will be easier to control.

In your early efforts you may have some trouble in gauging distance. That's natural. Judgment in estimating the yardage to the green comes with practice and experience. You can't get it overnight. Usually, at first, you will hit them short. Few pupils overshoot the green when they begin practicing this shot. But they are all afraid they will, and consequently ease up.

Concentrate on these short ones. The advice I gave you in discussing chip shots is still good: make up your mind how hard you are going to hit the ball in approach shots and then *stick to it*. If—as rarely happens—you hit the ball too far, make a mental note to take a shorter stroke next time.

As you move into approach shots of 50 to 100 yards, you will naturally be using a longer swing. But again keep in mind the tempo of the formula. Swing that club as fast as you can and still control it. Back and forth. Swing it away, hit it. A faint heart never won a fair lady, nor sank an approach shot. Swing it away, hit it. One-and-two.

Remember that follow-through. After your club hits the ball, keep that left arm straight and let the club keep right on going. Get a nice, high finish. I'd rather see a student get a good high finish to his shot than anything else. It means he took a clean shot, well balanced and decisive throughout the entire swing.

If you run into any trouble on these approach shots—dubbing, topping, slicing, hooking—glance back to the end of the chapter on chip shots. The same faults in approach shots and chip shots require the same remedies.

Occasionally—at least once on every average golf course—you will have one extremely short hole. The distance from tee to cup will be within the range of the approach clubs. Play these exactly like any other approach shot, except that from the teeing spot you can—and should—use a wooden tee.

One of the commonest playing errors made by the average golfer is failing to use a tee when a drive with an iron is called for. A tee simplifies the problem of getting the ball into the air.

60

It gives the golfer confidence. When you get down to the professional scoring range you can throw your tees away on tee shots, but until then you'll find it advisable to tee up your ball.

Tee up the ball for these short irons about a quarter inch. Then, in the same confident, decisive stroke that you use for other approach shots aim for the cup.

These holes are usually surrounded by more than a normal amount of hazards. Remember that hazards are designed to worry you. The timid player gets concerned when confronted by water holes or deep sand traps. He tightens up and the tension causes a dubbed shot.

You can overcome this obstacle by keeping mental notes on the distances you get with various clubs. Assuming you hit an average ball with a No. 7 iron a distance of 120 yards, you have no problem with a short hole of 120 to 125 yards. The hazards all lie in front of where your ball will drop *if you take your usual swing.*

If you have such a short hole at your course, take your proper stance at the ball, line it up, and then forget about everything except hitting the ball. If you hit the ball right, the hazards aren't going to count anyway, so why worry about them. Concentrate on hitting the ball right. These holes give you plenty of opportunity for par or even one-under-par birdies. Take advantage of them.

Now let's take a quick review of your short game.

From the outer rim of the scoring zone—120 yards—use your No. 7 iron with a full swing. From 100 yards, your No. 8 iron is normally your best club. Your No. 9 iron will carry about 90 yards.

Within this area, up to shots just off the green, use your No. 7, 8, or 9 iron or a sand or pitching iron. Use the club with the lowest number—the least loft—wherever possible. Hence your No. 7 iron ought to be your choice under most circumstances. However, where you need to hit a ball with less roll, choose one of your other irons. The No. 8 for a medium roll, the No. 9 for less roll, and the sand or pitching iron for hitting a ball that you want to stop pretty dead when it lands.

Then, in very close, you are in chipping area. Here again you want, wherever possible, to use the club with the least loft—the No. 5 iron. Use a No. 6 for a medium roll and the No. 7 for a very short roll.

HOW TO USE YOUR IRONS

The sketch in the upper left hand corner shows the three-quarter swing with an iron. A full iron shot would, of course, be longer, but never quite so long as a full swing with the driver. The club travels in the same path as the full swing, but it is used for shots requiring less distance and more control.

The center sketch shows the same pose from a different angle. The principles are the same for all swings. The left heel has left the ground slightly, causing a slight break in the left knee. The right elbow is pointing down toward the hip pocket.

The upper right-hand sketch may help you visualize the difference in clubs. Here I am holding a No. 5 iron. Notice how much closer I am to the ball than I would be with the driver. Note the difference in the position of the hands. With even shorter irons, of course, the ball would be even closer to my feet.

The lower left-hand sketch shows the long iron from the golfer's eye level and the lower right-hand sketch, the short iron. Note the difference in stance, the position of the ball. For the long irons, you use a slightly closed stance with the ball played off the left instep. For the short irons, the stance is slightly open.

Note that in all shots the hands are ahead of the ball.

Don't sell yourself short on the short ones. It is the best spot for all golfers—men and women—to cut down their strokes.

Fill in score card 4 on the front end leaves. From inside the scoring zone (120 yards out from the green) aim to take no more than three strokes to sink the ball. If you can drop it in with two strokes, you are moving into the expert class.

Three strokes give you a lot of leeway. It gives you three possible combinations. (1) Hitting the green and taking two putts. (2) Hitting the edge of the green, one chip, and one putt. (3) One long approach, one short approach shot, and one putt.

If you are taking four or more shots, better practice.

10 CUTTING DOWN YOUR IRON SHOTS

A FEW YEARS AGO two golfers got into an argument at the Dubs-dread Course at Orlando, Florida. They disagreed on the number of strokes they had taken. The squabble got more and more heated. Finally, armed with a driver, an iron and twenty-four balls, the pair paced off 50 yards. At a signal they began swinging.

Several shots were wide, then one antagonist knocked his opponent down with a shin drive. Then he started taking his eye off the ball and his shots went wild. Three shots later his enemy knocked him down with one to the ribs. Suddenly the golf duel ended. The cops had arrived.

I presume you will never get into such a position. But you will want to do your sharpshooting on the golf course with the putting green as your target.

The irons are the sharpshooting clubs. They are also the trouble clubs. Except in rare cases, they are the clubs to use when your ball strays off the fairway and into the thick grass of the rough. On the fairway the irons, having more loft, will get the ball into the air and will give the ball enough "bite" to halt the roll. Having shorter shafts, they are, generally speaking, easier to handle than the woods.

We have already discussed the No. 7, 8, and 9 irons and the sand pitching irons. And we have talked of the No. 5, 6, and 7 irons as chipping irons. Now we will discuss the long and medium irons—Numbers 1, 2, 3, 4, 5, and 6 irons as they are used beyond the scoring zone.

Each club, for the average player, adds 10 yards of distance. Thus, here is the chart for the average player:

No.	Yards
6	130
5	140
4	150
3	160
2	170
1	180

The average player ordinarily will not carry the No. 1 iron (the driving iron). More likely he will have a No. 2 or 3 wood (spoon), which we will discuss a little later in the book.

As we move outside the scoring zone, there will be one major change in your game. With the short irons and approach and chip shots, we took a stance with the left foot back about an inch farther from the line of flight than the right.

Now we take a different stance. For the No. 1, 2, 3, 4, 5, 6 irons, the *right* foot should be about an inch farther back from the line of flight than the left. In other words, just the opposite from the stance for short irons.

Let me explain briefly the reason for the change in stance. For the short shots the feet were relatively close together, the ball was played near the feet, and most of the work was done by the arms and hands.

As we move into the longer shots, the feet will be farther apart. The pivot will be greater. There will be more power. The force of the body uncoiling becomes more and more important as we progress into the longer shots.

Whereas with the short shots the club head traveled in a rather upright plane, with the longer irons the path will be flatter. By this I mean you stood nearly upright and the path of the club head was nearly upright. The path of the club, taken by a motion-picture camera, would show a hooplike path only slightly tilted back. With the longer shots, the hoop will be tilted farther back. I'll go into more detail in the chapter on "The Perfect Golf Swing."

But the important thing is that with the right foot slightly back, the club head will come in on an angle at the ball. This angle will be from inside the line of flight as it passes your left foot and outside the line of flight as you make your follow-through. This is the so-called "inside-out" swing.

This will give a slight spin to the ball, causing a slight draw or hook to the left. This also helps you to avoid the common error of slicing.

As you recall, with the chip shot your feet were very close together. With the approach shots, your stance was a little wider. Now, as you get into the longer irons your stance will be still a little bit wider. With each successive club, your stance will widen slightly. Your feet will be a bit farther apart with the No. 5 iron than with the No. 6, and so on. This, as with all your stances, is only a guide. It is up to you to decide the stance that gives you the best results and that is the most comfortable.

The ball is played from a position even with your left instep.

Let's familiarize ourselves with each of the irons.

Start with the No. 6 iron. Take the proper stance, right foot slightly back of the left, your feet slightly farther apart than in the approach shots. Remember the grip and the sitting-down position. The club shaft and left arm form approximately a straight line. The hands (from eye level) are ahead of the ball.

Keeping the wrists straight, practice the formula, first with a one-foot backswing. One, two, three, SWING! Practice this short swing for a while until you get the feel of the club. Then gradually lengthen the backswing. When you have the feel of the full swing, take the simpler rhythm of swing it away, hit it!

Always keep two things in mind.

1. The quickie rhythm. One-and-two. Swing it away, hit it!

2. The object of the swing always is to return the club head to the precise spot from which it began in back of the ball.

Repeat the process with the No. 5 iron.

Then the No. 4.

Next, the No. 3.

Then, the No. 2 iron, and (if you have one) the No. 1 iron.

Take time to get acquainted with each club, first using the short backswing, then gradually lengthening your swing.

Concentrate on starting your swing right. Move the club away with your wrists straight—the shoulders, arms, hands, and club moving as one unit. If you are encountering a slice with these clubs, you are likely to find your fault either in the grip or in a failure to start your swing properly.

You will also have to be careful of the firmness of your grip. This is particularly true when hitting out of the heavy rough. The club head will encounter the resistance of the grass and finally the impact of the club striking the ball. If you don't have a firm grip, the club is likely to turn in your hands and result in a muffed shot.

Let me issue another warning. Some beginners attempt to add yardage to their club by slugging at the ball. Every now and then it may work. But most times slugging will destroy your timing and balance, and the club face is likely to meet the ball at a bad angle.

Learn your distances with each club and stick to them. As your tempo speeds up and your timing improves, you will add distance. But you will add it *naturally* and consistently. An occasional extra-long shot isn't worth losing a dozen other strokes for. That's the usual penalty for trying to kill the ball.

Ordinarily there will be several short holes on your course where you will use an iron for your tee shot. You should always tee up the ball.

As you will learn in more detail during the next chapter on driving, the use of the tee raises the ball from its normal position. This means the arc of your swing must also be raised slightly to properly contact the ball.

And here again resist the temptation to slug the ball. Learn— as the professionals say—to play "within yourself." Know your own game—and then apply it to the golf course. There is a great tendency among golfers to ignore these middle shots with the long and medium irons, possibly because these shots lack the distance of the woods and don't require quite the pin-point precision of the short irons.

But a stroke lost anywhere on the course is adding to your score. So aim for a well-balanced game by giving plenty of thought to your irons. Because, likewise, a shot saved with the irons is a stroke taken off your score.

11 DRIVING FOR DISTANCE

IN 1945 a farmer near Columbus, Ohio, came into court. He wanted $25,000 damages from the owners of the Bridgeview Golf Course which adjoined his property. "Forty per cent of the balls off the first tee went wild," the farmer protested. They landed in his yard and scared off all his animals, he claimed.

The owners of the club were also unhappy. They wanted back the 3,500 golf balls he had hoarded. The golfers asserted that there was little wonder that they sliced. The farmer, they said, stood alongside his fence and heckled them as they prepared to drive. That rattled them. And, in addition, they said he built smudge fires on his property so the smoke obscured the fairways.

Golf faults for the average player are usually most noticeable in driving. Driving requires a power club with a long swing and plenty of distance to the flight of the ball. If you have a tendency to slice it will be most noticeable—and most disastrous—in driving. That is the reason I have taken you up through the shorter clubs first. You have now had opportunity to develop your swing and timing in preparation for their greatest test: driving.

There is always a lot of discussion among golf instructors as to which shot they consider the most important. Actually, of course, they all are.

A poor tee shot is not fatal because you can make a recovery shot and often be just as far along. But it is certainly helpful to get started right. A good shot from the tee sets you up well.

If you have developed your game consistently to this point, you should have little trouble with driving. You have become accustomed to the hand action and the right feel of the properly executed shot. This—with all clubs—is the mark of the good golfer.

In making the transition from irons to the driver, suppose you follow a procedure I have found most helpful in teaching my pupils to drive.

Pick up your No. 7 iron and take the proper stance. Now do the formula, starting first with the short backswing. One, two, three, SWING! Gradually lengthen your backswing until you are taking a full swing at the ball.

Now, pick up your driver. You will notice immediately that the club head feels heavier and its longer shaft means a longer swing. But the principles of the swing are just the same.

Take a wide stance with your driver. A safe rule for most golfers is to place their feet about as wide apart as their shoulders. Again, as I have explained in earlier chapters, this is simply a guide. By practice you will learn the best stance for your game.

Your feet will be in relatively the same position as they were for the long irons. Your right foot will be about an inch farther from the line of flight than your left. Your toes should be pointing outward.

The ball, as in the medium and long iron shots, will be played off your left instep. And, of course, it will be teed up. On that point, let me pause just a moment to encourage you to tee your ball up properly. About a half inch, or the width of your forefinger and middle finger, is the best height.

The other points of the stance which have already been discussed are true of the drive. And, if anything, they are more important. That means that you should remember to bend those knees—the sitting-down motion. Feel that you are sitting down with the upper part of your body. Relax your knees but still feel that you are standing erect. Most golfers, as a matter of fact, will stand more erect with the driver than with the shorter-shafted irons.

The bent knees are very vital in the drive because of the tremendous power involved. Your weight should, as always, be back on your heels to give you perfect balance throughout the swing.

Likewise, as in the other shots, your weight should be evenly balanced between your right and left feet.

Take your proper stance for driving. With your wrists straight, move the driver back two or three feet and then return it to the ball.

Notice one change over the previous clubs. Since your ball is teed up, the club should start at tee height (about a half inch). Your object in the drive is to pick the ball off the tee as cleanly as possible. Hitting underneath the ball will rob you of much-needed power and distance.

And so—always remembering that the theory behind a golf swing is to return the club face to its original position—as you start the club back it should be at the proper height to hit the ball squarely.

Try it a few times until you become accustomed to the feel of striking the ball, not off the ground, but off the tee.

Don't worry if you are erratic at this point. Everybody is. Just keep the point in mind and gradually you will accustom your swing to this new arc.

Let's go to work. With the decisive quickie rhythm take your driver back three to four feet and return it to the ball. Repeat. Repeat again. And now, hit the ball. One, two, three, SWING! One, two, three, SWING!

You won't get quite the speed now that you had with the short No. 7 iron, but always be seeking to speed up that rhythm—the faster the better, as long as you keep control over the club. You will probably take longer to learn my exercise with the driver. The heavier, longer driver takes more time to get used to.

Let's try it again. One, two, three, SWING!

The arms and hands and club head should all be moving back as one unit, guided by the turn of the shoulders. This means the wrists and arms are straight inside the hitting area. It guarantees that you are not cocking the wrists too soon on the way back or too late on the downswing—both disastrous golf troubles. It means you are swinging the club back, instead of picking it up.

One, two, three, SWING!

Notice the importance of having the weight evenly divided between the two feet and the reason that they should be well spread

THE CORRECT BACKSWING

Sketch 1 shows the proper starting position for a drive. Note that the knees are relaxed, weight evenly divided and back on the heels. This same position from eye level is shown in the center sketch. The drawing shows a square stance; however, most golfers will find a slightly closed stance preferable. Note that the hands are gripping the club properly and are slightly ahead of the ball.

The second sketch shows the start of the backswing. The club has been swung back with the single movement of shoulders turning, arms and club together. Note how low to the ground the club head is—an essential to the properly grooved swing.

Farther in the backswing, as shown in the lower left hand sketch, the centrifugal force of the swing has started the cock of the wrists. The shoulders are well turned; the hips have turned; the left heel has left the ground slightly and the left knee is bent somewhat toward the right leg.

In the final sketch, the golfer has reached the top of his backswing. Note that the right elbow is pointing down toward the hip pocket; the right hand is under the shaft. Notice also the perfect balance, the feeling of control over the club.

and with the weight back on the heels. You need a good foundation, and good balance, to obtain a good co-ordinated movement.

Now let's try a little longer backswing. Still with the same rhythm. Wrists straight. Arms, hands, and club moving as a single unit. One, two, three, SWING! One, two, three, SWING! The club starting and finishing so as to hit the ball neatly off its tee.

All right. Take a short rest while we talk some theory on driving. Did you notice how low to the ground the club head traveled during that short, fast backswing? That is the sign of a good start. It means that you are properly taking the club back with the pivot of the shoulders carrying the arms, hands, and club. I have stressed this point frequently during the formula exercises. You will also find this advice repeated later in the book in the section on "Curing Your Faults." The reason: In my experience I have found that a failure to swing the club away on the backswing is an important factor in producing golf faults. Picking the club up with a conscious cocking of the wrists destroys the natural swing and makes it very difficult to bring the club back down in the proper groove.

It will make my teaching job easier—and your golf game better —if you will concentrate on this "swing it away" phase now, rather than wait until we have to help you overcome your golf faults.

If your club head isn't traveling low to the ground, better stop and take notice. Recheck the very start of your backswing.

Here's a tip I have found helpful to my pupils.

Feel the base of the club scrape the ground for at least two feet at the start of the backswing. If your club skims the ground for that distance it will be started on the right arc.

The natural swing, following that groove on the downswing, thus will come in to strike the ball at a low angle—sweeping the ball off the tee.

As your backswing gets longer, notice the path of the club. It is moving past your right foot, striking the ball, and continuing on. The club cuts across the line of flight on an outward angle. This means an "inside-out" swing that produces a slight hook that in turn means maximum yardage for your drive.

Try a little longer backswing now. One, two, three, SWING!

Notice as you swing the club back rapidly how the left knee follows by moving in toward the right leg. That's the factor that many instructors make such a fuss about. Sure, you are shifting your weight to the right. But why worry about it? With speed in your swing, that knee movement just happens. You don't have to think about it. Just swing that club; the weight shift will take care of itself.

As your club sweeps the ball away, notice how your club flies on at an outward angle. Let it fly without trying to stop it short. With your left arm straight, the club head weight will carry your hands nice and high for the right finish to your swing. It will pull your shoulders around *naturally* so you face the hole at the end of your swing. It will also pull your head up at the right time.

As you reach the limit of your swing with wrists straight, notice how your backswing pulls your left foot over on its side and up on the toe. I call your attention to it, not so that you will become aware of it, but only that you will not resist that natural movement. Let it happen.

Now, keeping up that one-two-three-swing rhythm, extend your swing farther by cocking your wrists. This again will be a natural movement as you swing that club back rapidly.

Much as I dislike the use of the word "don't," I'll have to use it here.

The function of the formula lies in these principles:

1. The wrists should be straight at the start of the backswing and as the club head returns to meet the ball. That's the reason for the straight-wrist exercise. It trains the hands for the feel of the club and for the feel of the proper position at the time of striking the ball.

2. Speed in backswing and downswing. The one-and-two rhythm. The "swing it away, hit it" tempo. Combined with the straight-wrist exercise in the hitting area and a proper stance at the start of your swing, speed makes all the rest of the bodily movements come naturally. It helps you create a smooth, even swing.

There are speed, action, life in that swing instead of the tension of a slow-motion golfer like Danny.

So—and here is my "don't"—don't destroy the effectiveness of the formula by trying to interject your own ideas into the swing. Don't think to yourself, "Now is the time for me to shift my weight, now is the time to cock my wrists, now is the time to start my downswing, now is the time to uncock my wrists, now is the time to raise

SWING IT AWAY!

Here is how the backswing looks from the front view. Observe the proper stance, correct weight distribution, and the relaxed knees. The correct start in the golf swing is most important.

In the upper right-hand sketch, the golfer has *swung* the club away with a spontaneous turn of the shoulders; arms, hands, and club moving together. Note that the club head is low to the ground. This will aid in bringing about the proper turn of the body during the backswing.

Using just the two sketches at the top of the page, you can practice the Revolta formula for the driver. Simply transpose these positions onto the earlier page illustrating the Revolta formula and practice the one-two-three-SWING exercise.

In the bottom right-hand sketch, the club has reached the spot where the swing has caused the wrists to begin to cock. Note from the small inserted sketch how the swinging movement has caused the left heel to leave the ground and the foot to turn over slightly. This shows the maximum movement of this foot during any swing.

In the lower left-hand sketch is the top of the backswing. The club is horizontal to the ground, the club face is pointing at a 45-degree angle toward the ground. Note that the shoulders are fully turned and the head is still pointing toward the ball. The inserted sketch shows the proper position of the left hand. Note the creases at the wrist, which appear when the club is properly held.

my head," and so on. The swing is over in a fraction of a second. You don't have time to think about all those things. If you think about one factor in the swing, you'll forget about the others.

Instead, rely on speed and the straight-wrist exercise. Let your body flow with the clubhead back on the backswing and forward on the downswing.

Now, if you've taken the club back far enough so that your wrists naturally cock, your club head on the downswing will fly through the ball and on past. As I mentioned earlier, let the club head fly. It will travel outward and upward. Keep your left arm straight until your hands are way up high. Then fold your arms down to take up the last of the club head speed. You will find this motion occurs naturally if you don't consciously try to stop your follow-through.

A good test of the follow-through is whether you feel the end of that swing in the small of your back. If you let that club fly and your hands finish high, it will pull your body up high and you'll feel a tug down in the small of your back. That means you are finishing correctly.

Mayor Martin Kennelly of Chicago once asked me the single most important thing in a golf swing. I told him I thought a good finish was the most important—and here's why. If you finish high, it is almost a sure thing that you have swung back and through the ball properly. And that, friends, is all there is to a good swing.

Now, forget the one-two-three-SWING tempo for the moment.

Instead simply take the club back and then down to strike the ball. Swing it away, hit it! One-and-two. Finish high—the higher the better. Let that club head really fly. Be sure you haven't forgotten to keep those knees bent in the sitting-down position as you take your stance. That's essential to the smooth-flowing swing. Swing it away—hit it! At the top of your follow-through, fold those arms and collapse your wrists. And feel that follow-through in the small of your back.

Take time out every few shots to practice our exercise with the one-two-three-SWING rhythm using a short one- or two-foot backswing. That's the hitting area that dictates which way and how neatly you clip the ball off the tee. Mix up the long swing and the short ones. Every time you swing you are training your hands to feel the right shot.

About this time it is a good idea to look at your stance. Are you comfortable? If not—if you feel tense—check your feet position and posture. I told you earlier that a good stance for most golfers is with feet about shoulder-width apart. For most, it gives a good solid base for a quick swing and enough freedom for you to follow the natural flow of the swing. Some golfers, however, will prefer a wider stance; others feel more comfortable with their feet slightly closer together.

Lloyd Mangrum, for example, is one of the country's outstanding golfers. His feet are quite close together. Ben Hogan on the other hand has a wide stance.

There is another factor to consider in your drive. And that is the extent and arc of your swing.

In the second chapter I made the point that many golf books attempt to teach the upright swing, which is not suited to most golfers. There is nothing wrong with an upright swing. As a matter of fact, it is the swing used by many of our greatest tournament players.

But it is in trying to imitate that upright swing that the average golfer goes haywire.

The upright swing is what its name implies. The club head in all stages of the backswing stays relatively close to the line of flight. On the other hand a flat swing will be more of a shoulder turn.

The average golfer, in attempting to swing upright, invariably does this. He starts the club head back along the line of flight properly for about three feet. But then he pulls the club upward. His right elbow goes out on a backward angle—which is wrong. In the upright swing the hands are very high at the top of the backswing. The average golfer, in imitating this swing, is likely to dip his body to exaggerate this stretching motion.

Another very common fault in imitating this swing is to fail to turn the shoulders. After the golfer takes the club back part way, instead of carrying the club back with a turn of the shoulders, he pulls it up with his arms.

The normal result of these errors is a badly sliced ball.

The experts, of course, do not make these errors. They use the upright swing, but they use it properly. Very few beginners can.

That is why I have advocated that you use a flatter swing. If

79

THE DOWNSWING

Notice first the middle sketch. This shows the golfer at the start of his golf swing. In the previous pages of illustrations, the golfer swung the golf club back.

Now, in the top sketch he has swung the club back down. This golfer has rebalanced his feet and is now firmly set to hit the ball. But his hands are still coiled.

The middle picture now shows the golfer as he hits the ball, an exact copy of the position he had when he started his swing. Notice what has happened to his hands in both pictures. They have uncoiled in the hitting area. That is what I mean by hand action. You can just see the snap, firmness, and control of those hands as they bring the club down to send the ball far down the fairway.

In the following sketch the centrifugal force of the club head speed has carried the arms straight through. The right side of his body is following the turn. During this split second the head begins to lift to follow the flight of the ball.

IN ALL OF THESE SKETCHES BEWARE OF A COMMON PUPIL FAULT. DON'T TRY TO IMITATE THE POSITIONS CONSCIOUSLY. DON'T STUDY THEM AND THEN TRY TO CONTORT YOURSELF INTO THESE POSES. The purpose of these sketches is simply to show you what happens when you swing properly by following the instructions I have given. Only the trained golf instructor can consciously break his swing into these stages; so don't you try. Follow the lessons carefully and your swing will fit these illustrations.

you have followed my instructions faithfully, you will have this type of swing.

The secret of this flatter, and more natural, swing lies in starting your backswing with the turn of the shoulders, and in keeping the club head low to the ground. With that decisive tempo— one-and-two—your shoulders simply have to turn properly.

Also you will find it almost impossible not to have your right elbow in its proper position—which is pointing almost straight down at your right back pocket.

The arc of the swing travels low at the start and then moves upward, with the result that at the top of the backswing the wrists are cocked fully. Your left wrist is cocked upward and back and you will notice that creases, or wrinkles, form where the wrist joins the hand just below the base of the thumb. The back of the left hand will be almost straight up and down at the top of the back-swing.

With this flatter swing, your club shaft at the top of your backswing will be pointing upward at an angle. It will probably be about two-thirds of the way around from straight up and down to the horizontal.

As you practice, however, and get more speed in your swing, you will find that your hands go higher and you get a shade more turn at the waist and shoulders. This will lengthen your swing and you will find that your club, at the top of your backswing, is now horizontal with the ground.

This horizontal swing is known among professionals as a short swing. This is the swing that I use. My club shaft never dips below the horizontal. Some other professionals do use a longer swing and their club at the top of their backswing is pointing downward.

Some professionals use the short swing normally; but, in emergencies when they need extra yardage, they add that extra leverage to their swing. I have seen Ben Hogan, for example, get an extra fifty yards on his drive by carrying his club back farther on his backswing.

For all except top professionals, however, I believe the short swing is far superior. It gives better control and its speed makes up for the loss of that extra leverage. The longer swing is slower.

In addition many students fall into the error of lengthening their backswing by loosening their hold on the club at the top of their backswing. This robs them of control over the club. Generally speaking, I have found the shorter swing more adaptable to most of my pupils. It lends itself to the quickie rhythm and to control.

But this decision must be yours. However, if you use the longer swing and find your shots scattering erratically around the fairways, shorten up, because that will mean you have no control over the club. Also, if you are a woman golfer, nearly every time you will find the shorter swing better.

Now, if you have your swing with the driver working right, you have gained a new feel for your clubs and a better understanding of the factors in the Revolta exercise.

So, you may find it helpful to go back through all your clubs trying the exercise again. On the shorter irons, of course, the momentum of the swing will not carry the club so far on the follow-through.

Also, with the irons you will never take quite so long a backswing as with the driver. With the irons the backswing should not fall below the horizontal.

Go right through your bag of clubs. Concentrate always on bringing the club head back to the ball in the same position from which it started. I call that process "re-timing" your club head. Get your weight set right. Concentrate on the quickie rhythm. Concentrate on getting the feel of the right swing—train your hands to know good golf.

If the ball flies squarely toward your target, well and good. If it has a tendency to hook or slice, don't worry about it. About one out of ten players has this problem at this stage of his lessons. But it's easy to cure. We'll clean up that problem in a later chapter on curing your faults.

For most players, however, hitting the ball squarely and with the smooth flowing swing of the formula means a ball flying far and true. And you are off to lower and lower scores.

The next time out keep a special record on your drives on score card 5 on the front end leaves. Mark them up for distance and accuracy. This will provide a check to help you decide whether you need more work on this department.

Use this code to simplify your scoring: "S" for straight; "H" for hooked; "SL" for sliced; "T" for topped; "W" for wild, on shots that traveled straight but went off on a wild angle.

FOLLOWING THROUGH

In the previous sketches in this chapter we have traced the backswing and the downswing. In the last illustration the club had just passed the point of impact.

In these drawings we see the final stages of the follow-through.

In the upper left-hand corner the golfer has reached the place where his wrists are beginning to fall over. His head is responding to the natural pull of the swing and he is following the flight of the ball.

In the upper right-hand corner the follow-through is nearly complete. Notice that the head is now nearly straight, the arms are "giving" at the elbows. The golfer has turned to face the hole, in the natural turning movement of the correct swing. Note particularly that the hands are high, one of the important tests of a good follow-through.

The two sketches at the bottom of the page show the completion of the golf swing. The golfer is now turned to face the hole, his hands are high, his head is up. Notice particularly in these sketches that the golfer is in perfect balance at every point in the golf swing. This is the result of starting right, swinging the club, and good footwork.

12 GETTING TO THE GREEN

ONCE you are off the tee with your drive but with still plenty of distance to the green, your fairway woods come into play. On the fairway with a clean shot at the ball, woods are preferable because they give you more yardage than irons.

These clubs include the No. 2, 3, 4, and 5 woods.

The No. 2 has been the object of more than its share of profanity. And, I think, with justification. It is the most difficult club in the bag for most players. It is heavy and hard to control.

For that reason many professionals have rejected the club for all except occasional shots. I seldom use one. I would advise most players to forget about the No. 2 and concentrate on the No. 3, 4, and 5 woods.

You can get almost as much distance with a No. 3 wood (the spoon) and it is much easier to use. For one thing it has more loft and it is easier to get the ball into the air. It is lighter and more easily controlled. There are very few times when a spoon won't do just as well as a No. 2—and do it a lot easier.

So when we talk about fairway woods, let's confine our thinking to the spoons—the No. 3, 4, and 5 woods. The No. 3 wood will carry about 190 yards; the others slightly less.

The No. 3 wood is your all-round fairway club. Most golfers have confidence in this club and—with a small amount of practice —you will too. The same principles employed with the driver are true of the spoon. Start the club back with a turn of the shoulders, carrying the arms, straight wrists, and club in one unit. And don't forget the quickie rhythm.

Like the drive, it is played off the left instep with feet evenly balanced, weight back on the heels, and the right foot slightly farther back than the left.

As with the other clubs, take plenty of time to learn your woods through the Revolta exercise. Start out first with a two- or three-foot backswing, and then gradually lengthen the backswing as you get the proper feel of the club.

Once you have left the teeing area, of course, you have to play the ball from where it lies. Don't forget to adjust your aim, once more, to picking the ball off the ground instead of off the tee.

Swing it away—hit it! And watch it sail for distance.

If, as in my note in the chapter on driving, you find a hook or slice, don't worry about it. We'll get rid of it promptly in the lesson on curing your faults. But concentrate on your grip, stance, straight wrists at the start, quickie rhythm, and the good follow-through. We'll iron out any minor problems later.

The No. 3 wood is good only on the fairway, although on some short holes you may find it suitable as a driver. But it requires a clean shot at the ball. Heavy grass that muffles the impact rules out this club. Better reach for an iron.

The No. 4 or 5 wood, however, can be used in the light rough. Having knoblike heads, these woods will slide through grass that is not too thick.

They are handled just like their partner, the No. 3 wood. They simply have more loft and will get the ball higher into the air than any of the other woods. So you'll get a good high shot and still have plenty of distance. They are handy clubs, and worth having, if they are not now in your set. But for the average player only one of these two clubs will be necessary.

Common faults with fairway wood shots are topping the ball or hitting the ground behind the ball. The cure lies in slowly progressing through the exercise with gradually longer backswings. As I advised with the driver, spend a good deal of time with the short backswing exercise to perfect the feel inside the hitting area. That's the best way to avoid running into trouble with your fairway woods.

13 GETTING OUT OF TRAPS EASILY

IN THE 1948 National Amateur tournament at Memphis, Richard Ewert sent his fourteenth hole drive into a sand trap. He took his stance for a shot, when suddenly a newspaper photographer cried out: "Don't shoot. I can't see the ball."

"That's all right," shrugged Ewert. "Neither can I."

The shot traveled only a few feet, so did the second, and the next arched into a ditch. When the next shot skidded clear across the green, Ewert took the hint and conceded the hole.

On the eighteenth his opponent, Skee Riegel, ran into similar trouble. His second shot hit sand, and his recovery arched over the green into the far sand trap. He finally holed a fifteen-footer for a bogey 5. But Ewert blew his chance for a tie when he missed an easy three-foot putt.

Interestingly enough, it was sand traps that finally settled the outcome of that tournament.

Willie Turnesa, the youngster in that famous golfing family, emerged champion, 2 and 1, in a thirty-six-hole match. Ten times —seven from sand and three from gullies, he used the sand iron to flip the ball onto the green—and eventual victory.

Willie would have nothing to do with that club until ten years earlier, just before the 1938 tournament. He regarded it as a mongrel until he stopped at the Winged Foot Club and saw a friend trying one out. Twice this friend holed out from traps.

Willie decided to give it a try and bought one from Craig Wood's shop—a woman's model. Shortly afterward he won the National Amateur from Buell Patrick Abbott. Pat said Turnesa was in bunkers at Oakmont fourteen times, yet he won easily 8 and 7.

Turnesa's own explanation of his later victory was this. "I was tired after the twenty-seventh hole and began to lose my concentration. I lost the next three holes and when I didn't drop a three footer on the thirtieth hole I knew I had to go back to work or be out."

Nor is Turnesa the only player who has found the sand iron a valuable club. It has knocked two strokes off the scores of professionals, accounting for some tournament scoring down in the 60's. For the average player it probably saves even more strokes.

The sand-trap shot is—and should be—the easiest shot in the bag.

There is more room for error in this shot than in any other. You can hit a half inch, an inch, or even two inches behind the ball and still be all right. With other shots, that margin of error would result in a bad shot.

An explosion shot out of a sand trap is easy with a No. 9 iron. With a sand iron this shot is a lead-pipe cinch.

If you don't already own a sand iron, by all means add it to your set. It has a heavy sole (bottom of the club head) which prevents its digging into the sand. It is heavy, so it encourages you to swing it and let the club do the work. It has plenty of loft to get the ball into the air.

If you do not yet own a sand iron, a No. 9 iron can produce fairly good results. If you have an older set of clubs, you may have a niblick. This club, similar to the present No. 9 iron, has somewhat the shape of the sand iron, but is not so heavy.

But the sand iron will give you the best results. It is especially designed for sand shots—and it requires little more for you to do than to hold on. It is also a handy gadget for approach shots, which we discussed earlier. For lower scores and for licking the sand traps, you can't make a better investment.

Ordinarily sand traps are located in two places—bordering the fairways between the tee and green or right around the putting

THE ABC OF PROPER STANCE FOR AN EXPLOSION

In sketch *A*, the golfer has taken his normal stance for an approach shot. Naturally, his feet are closer together than they would be in an explosion shot.

So first broaden your stance slightly.

In sketch *B* the golfer is still standing as in sketch *A*, but he has turned the club face open. This would knock the ball to the right of the pin.

In sketch *C* he has simply swung his body around to the left a little to bring the club face to point directly at the intended line of flight. Now the feet are quite open—more so than in any other shot—and the shoulders are open.

The ball is played well off the left foot. From the position shown in sketch *C*, swing the club back and straight through along the line of flight to the hole.

This adjustment in stance is designed to limit the turning movement of the body. This is turn makes the club head travel in an upright swing and to hit a descending blow through the ball.

91

green. Golfers just taking up the game often don't get into these bunkers because their shots are generally short enough to miss them. As your game gets better you'll find yourself in these traps fairly often. The fellows who lay out golf courses specifically locate these traps so as to catch the better golfer either when his shots go a little off line or when his fairway shots get enough distance to carry to the edge of the green. So don't overlook this phase of your game.

Beginners have a great fear of sand traps. I presume this is due to some mental quirk which ties up traps with the difficulties of the game. They try to roll the ball out with a putter, scoop it out with an iron—anything, in fact, just to get the ball out. And generally they wind up taking several strokes to do it.

There are, of course, all kinds of sand traps. Some are so shallow they are little more than dents in the fairways filled with sand. Others are so deep that you need a ladder to climb in and out of them. And there are those in between.

In some the sand is loose, and in other traps it is packed tight. Especially after a rain the sand is most likely to be packed hard in any trap.

In very loose sand, the ball occasionally will fall in with such force as to become partially buried. Sometimes in demonstrations I take a golf ball and stamp on it so that it is completely buried and then blast it out onto the green. You are not likely to encounter that tough a problem. But I have found it an effective means of showing what can be done with an explosion shot.

Occasionally—but very rarely—a chip shot or an approach shot, just as those we did earlier off the grass—are feasible out of a sand trap. These few possibilities exist when you have a shallow bunker. Sometimes a professional, gambling, may even use a No. 4 wood out of a shallow bunker for a long shot.

But I can't advise gambling for the average player. The odds are too much against him. In at least 90 per cent of the cases, the explosion shot is the surest, safest, and best way out of sand.

And—with the sand iron—the easiest.

A very open stance is needed for an explosion shot. The left foot will be drawn back even farther from the line of flight than it was in the chip and approach shots. The adjoining sketches show how to find the right stance.

Don't forget that simple method. Take your approach stance; then shift the club face slightly back and readjust your grip. Rearrange your stance so that the club face is square to the hole. Then follow with your natural swing. Seemingly you will be aiming to the left of the cup as you swing, but don't worry about it. The maneuver will send the ball straight for the hole. Just follow your normal swing.

Let me encourage you to work on this explosion stance until you have it well in mind. Then work slowly through the Revolta exercise, gradually lengthening your backswing.

Sand, as you know, shifts. So it is especially important that you get your feet well anchored. As you take your proper stance, wiggle your feet until you get a good footing.

As in most other shots, you play the explosion off your left instep.

But—and this is an important difference—you aim for a spot just behind the ball instead of aiming to hit the ball itself.

The reason is that you want to hit the sand before the ball. Your club face hits first the sand and then the ball. The sand acts as a cushion. Actually the force of the blow drives the sand against the ball and the pressure pops it out onto the green.

For this reason don't be afraid to hit it too hard. The sand will deaden most of the force and leave just enough to toss the ball out onto the green.

In getting ready for your shot, take your proper stance for an explosion. Then pick the spot you want to hit in the sand—about a half inch to an inch behind the ball—and aim for it. It is against the rules to ground your club in the sand and mark your spot, so it will take a little practice to adjust your sights.

But, remember, you don't have to worry. You have plenty of room to hit and still make a good explosion shot.

Using my system for getting out of traps, you will find it easy whether the sand is fluffy or packed hard—whether your ball is lying on top or buried in the sand. If the ball is buried deeply, just aim a little farther behind and put a little more speed in your swing.

Where then does Danny the Duffer go wrong? He makes his error in failing to have confidence in his club. The sand iron is designed to get the ball out of sand. It has the heavy flange to

93

THE EXPLOSION SHOT

Here we see the golfer actually making an explosion shot.

The sketches are drawn from the front view and may not appear to show the open stance and open position of the body as demonstrated in the previous series of sketches.

Let's start with the middle sketch, which is actually the starting position. Note the stance, which is slightly wider than for other short shots.

The top sketch shows the maximum backswing for an explosion shot. The body has moved but little. Swinging the club away in an upright swing, described previously, has resulted in practically no pivot.

The middle sketch now represents the position of the body as the club head strikes behind the ball. When you look at these sketches, train your mind to recognize that this is both the starting position and the position at the moment of impact.

The bottom sketch shows the proper follow-through. The club head has swung through the ball and on, just as in any other shot. But this is one of the most difficult points of golf for most pupils. Either they scoop at the ball and the club gets buried in the sand so there is no force to carry the club through. Or they try to lift the ball by tilting their body back on their right foot. This could be described as "falling back" from the ball on the follow through.

LET THE CLUB DO THE WORK. The proper stance will produce an upright swing that lets the loft of the club lift the ball out of the sand and onto the green. Study particularly the bottom sketch. Learn to finish an explosion shot in the same manner as approaches and other shots. It will make the explosion one of your best, and easiest, shots.

keep from being buried. It has a big club face to give you plenty of hitting surface. It has a lot of loft to get the ball into the air. Everything is built into the club.

Danny the Duffer, however, doesn't trust his club. He wants to help get the ball into the air. He scoops at the ball. As a result the club either digs into the sand or he tops the ball. And it is still in the sand trap.

Trust your club to do the job. For yourself, simply concentrate on swinging it properly.

This shot to be effective has to travel through the sand and emerge in the normal fashion, just like any other swing. It can't hit into the sand and stay there. You can't hit down at the ball and have the club stop as it reaches the ball. It has to cut through, spraying sand, and follow on through.

Combined with chip shots, the average player will cut six to eight strokes off his score with good explosion shots. And there isn't anyone who wouldn't give plenty to knock his score down that much.

Now that you've gone through the full set of clubs, it is time to check up on your entire game on score card 6 on the back end leaves. Mark down each shot taken, using the letters for simplicity: "S" for straight, "H" for hooked, "SL" for sliced, "T" for topped, "W" for wild, and "D" for dubbed. Then, for your longer shots mark the estimated distance of the shot. As, for example, "S-200" for a straight 200 yard drive.

THINKING RIGHT

THUS FAR we have been concerned with the mechanics of the golf swing and the feel for the right shot.

Equally important is the mental side of golf: getting the right viewpoint of the game and of the individual shots; understanding what is taking place in the golf swing; and finally, understanding the reasons behind a shot that goes wrong.

In the next chapter, "How to Break 100," I will discuss the importance of "thinking right" on a golf course. Then, in the following chapter, "The Shots You Miss," I will show you the kind of shots that most golfers miss and their importance. It will give you a new insight into the right approach to rounding out your entire game.

Chapter 16 delves into the technical side of golf in explaining what makes shots go as they do and the mechanics behind a bad shot. This will then lead you into a chapter on "Curing Your Faults"—our golf laboratory in solving your golf problems.

Thinking right is essential to good golf.

So, for the moment, put aside your clubs while we do a little locker-room jawboning. . . .

14 HOW TO BREAK 100

CRAIG WOOD, one of the all-time greats in golfing, once took 11 strokes on a par-4 hole. Everybody wanted to know how that had happened. What had gone wrong. "Well," said Wood. "I had a long putt for a 10, but I missed."

Taking a big score on a hole happens to all of us, beginner and professional alike. The difference between the experienced and the inexperienced golfer, however, is that the pro can come back with par and below-par scores on subsequent holes and still turn in a good score. The beginner isn't likely to make that kind of recovery.

He has a limitation to his game. The golfer shooting around 120 is rarely down to par or one over par on any hole. His card is filled with 7's and 8's. The player whose score is a little better—somewhere around 110—is more likely to have 6's and 7's on his score card, an occasional par or one over par.

And most over-100 players are likely to have one or more bad holes on which they score a 9 or 10. If this score alone doesn't ruin their score, they are likely to complete the job by putting on the pressure to make up those lost strokes. Pressure means tension. Tension means more dubbed shots and a higher and higher score.

One reason for a golfer's shooting in the over-100 bracket is a lack of consistency in his game. He doesn't know how to use all his clubs properly. He hasn't spent sufficient time practicing my formula with each of his clubs.

But there is another reason for high scoring on a golf course. It is one that you can overcome as you sit in your home reading this book. It is a lesson that will assist you later on, when you are striving to break 90 and lower. It will help you avoid those holes where you "blow up" and take 9's and 10's.

It is simply to understand what you are up against on a golf course.

A golf professional will generally show up a day or so in advance of a tournament to play a few rounds. He wants to know what he is up against on that course. What is the layout? Where are the traps? What are the putting greens like? And he wants to test his own game against the course.

Then, immediately before he tees off during the match, the professional will spend an hour or more on the practice tee and putting green. Again checking his game. Going over his shots. Ironing out trouble spots.

Those are the things that matter to the player out to shoot par or subpar golf. They are equally important to all golfers. Learn the layout of your course. Practice.

But there is another factor, important to the average golfer. That is to cultivate your golf psychology. Get the right outlook. Learn to play within your own capabilities.

For example, there is the player who steps up to the first tee. The flag is 420 yards away. "Holy smokes!" he thinks. "That's a long way away." And subconsciously he thinks, "I've really got to hit this drive." He then proceeds to smack the ball with all his might. The usual result is a ball that slices or hooks badly. Or he tops it. Or he misses it altogether.

His outlook is all wrong. Sure, 420 yards is a long way—if you try to hit your drive all the way there. But 140 yards is not a long way. And three shots of 140 yards each will take you 420 yards to the green.

"But," protests the player. "Par on that hole is 4. I'd have to one-putt the green to make par."

Again his outlook is wrong. He isn't trying to shoot par. He is trying to break 100. That makes a big difference. He isn't trying

99

to shoot 72 for eighteen holes. He isn't ready for that yet. Nor is he ready to shoot par on any one of the eighteen holes.

His par is 100 for eighteen holes. He can do that by going *two* over course par on ten holes and one over par on eight holes in playing most courses.

So his goal on that 420-yard hole shouldn't be to shoot it in four. But to shoot it in five, or maybe six. That gives him three easy shots to reach the green and two, maybe three putts, for the 420-yard hole. And he is one-eighteenth of the way toward breaking 100.

This psychology will help the average golfer at another crucial point in his game. Let's say he messes up his drive. It goes slicing off into the rough a bare 100 yards from the tee. He walks over to locate his ball and then peers off into the distance at the green. It is a long way away—320 yards.

"I lost distance on my drive," thinks the golfer. "I gotta make it up on this shot." He is thinking of that par 4. He has already lost a stroke, which leaves him only three to sink the ball 320 yards away. He flails away trying to send the ball clear to the green. Result: another dubbed shot. Now instead of one error (his drive) his has two (a drive and a dubbed second shot) and he still isn't much closer to the green.

Again his outlook has gotten him into trouble. Suppose instead he had hit his second shot 100 yards and out on the fairway. And then he hits his third and fourth shots only 120 yards each. Then he sinks his ball in two putts. He has scored a 6, two over par. Which he can do on eight more holes and one-over-par on the rest and still break 100.

Actually the result is likely to be even more favorable. By having the right golf psychology—thinking in terms of three shots of 140 yards each, instead of one of 420 yards—his drive, instead of going 140 yards, will go farther. His second shot will be longer, and his third shot will be close enough to the green to give him a better shot for the pin.

And the same is true of the player with the right outlook whose previous shot has gone wrong. If he doesn't attempt to make up for his first error by vainly trying to pick up the lost yardage, he won't compound it into a second error and a jump in his score. He

may even be able to make it up on the fairway or putting green—
or on a later hole.

These two errors in psychology—that par is the goal for the
golfer trying to break 100; and the thought that you can make up
yardage on a lost shot—are two big reasons why golfers fail to break
100.

Take out the score card from your course and fill in score card
7 on the back end leaves. Where it says "Your Par" do this: Pick
out the ten toughest holes on your course. Add two strokes to the
number marked for par. On a par-3 hole *your* par will be 5; on
par-4's it will be 6; and on par 5's it will be 7. On the other eight
holes add one stroke to par. Now *your* par will be 4 on par 3's; 5 on
par 4's; and 6 on par 5's.

Now *your* par will add up to 100 on your course. This will
apply to courses where par is 72. If your course has a par of 73, you
will have one less hole where you can go two-over-par. Now you'll
have nine two-over-par holes and nine one-over-par holes. If your
course's par is 71, you'll have an extra two-over-par hole.

If you are striving to break 100, cross out the par figures on
your regular score card. That isn't meant for you—yet. Instead,
fill in the figures you have computed as *your* par. Now, if you can
beat *that* par you will break 100. That, after all, is your present
goal.

Sounds simple, doesn't it? Yet you will be surprised what a
difference it will make in your score. When you realize that you
have 6 strokes (instead of the 4 shown on the regular score card)
your task doesn't seem so difficult. It is easier to relax and play
your normal game. Trying to play with the pros when your score
is still over 100 can only mean that you are pressing and trying
to do the impossible.

Learn to play within your own capabilities. Using my system
for figuring par will help.

Keep this system flexible. Suppose you have marked the first
hole as one of your tough problems and you've given yourself two
extra strokes. If you save a stroke there as you play the first hole,
you have a bonus stroke. Add it right away to *your* par for the
next hole. If you again save it, add it to the third. And so forth
until you have played all eighteen holes.

Suppose, on the other hand, that you lose a stroke or so. Your score then goes over *your* par for that hole. Forget it. Don't add it to your problems by figuring you've got to make it up on the very next hole. That's like the fellow who tried to make up for a bad drive by pressing to hit the green on his next shot.

Just keep on playing for the par you've set for yourself. The odds are that you'll beat your par at a later hole and wipe out your earlier deficit.

Breaking 100 is easy. Let me prove it to you. Take the total yardage for your course. Allowing 2 putts a green, or 36 for eighteen holes, it leaves you 64 strokes to travel the fairways. Divide the total yardage of your course by 64. That shows you the distance your average shot has to travel. Isn't very far is it?

Just how easy it is for you to break 100 depends upon your ambitions in the game. And your abilities.

Let's take a look at your present game. How far can you drive? How far can you hit the ball with your other clubs?

What is your goal in golf? What score do you think you could make if you got rid of your faults? 100? 90? 80? Par?

You have to be realistic in setting this goal. It is obvious that you are not very likely to score below 90 if you can't drive a ball more than 150 yards. Your goal then ought to be to shoot in the 90's.

How often you can play and practice will also be a factor. If you cannot play and practice regularly, your game will take longer to improve. Your age and physical build will also be a factor in determining your goal. Your own ideas on golf also are important. Many golfers simply want to shoot respectable golf in the 90's. They can enjoy playing in that scoring bracket and have no particular desire to spend the time and effort needed to drop their score lower.

Take all those factors into consideration in evaluating your own game.

Of course the golfer who wants to shoot golf in the 90's can reach this goal more quickly and easily than the golfer whose eventual goal is to shoot in the 80's. He will be less demanding of getting distance in his drives and perfection in his other shots, and he can avoid a lot of errors his more ambitious counterpart will make.

If you want to break only 100—which most golfers do—concentrate on putting and in getting accuracy with your other shots. Spend most of your time practicing your putting. This is good advice for all beginners, but particularly is it true of this group of golfers. With your fairway shots, concentrate on accuracy. Content yourself with shorter shots, which you can control. Even if you can hit them farther, cut down your distance in favor of regular accuracy.

On an old score card from a championship course, I figured out that a golfer would not have to hit a single ball more than 116 yards and—if he hit each shot straight—he would break 100.

The player whose ambition is to shoot in the 80's and better, however, should *not* follow this course. He should not shorten his shots simply to gain accuracy. Instead, he should continue to hit the ball the way he does today, but aim to rid his game of errors. You cannot afford to shorten up your shots, if you are aiming for low scores. The reason: in shortening your shots, you will destroy the natural swing and timing needed for the longer shots.

Breaking 100 will require time and work. And patience. For it may take longer to break 100, but your game eventually will be superior to those who are content simply to shoot respectable golf.

There is, however, one way to speed up the process. That lies in concentrating on the shots you miss. Take plenty of time practicing and working on the shots that are giving you the most trouble. The Revolta exercise is usually the answer.

But now for a more detailed account of the shots you miss, turn the page.

15 THE SHOTS YOU MISS

In Tocopilla, a Chilean port, employees of a power plant laid out one of the world's most unusual golf courses. It lay amidst abruptly rising bluffs and its grounds were covered with huge jutting rocks. Only two clubs were needed to play the 3,500-yard course: a sand iron and a putter.

You will probably never encounter such a course. But wherever you play, you will use those clubs—the putter and short irons—more than any other clubs in your bag. They are the pay-off sticks —the clubs for playing in the scoring zone where golfers become either duffers or good players. It is in this area that women golfers must make up for their lack of distance in fairway shots. It is here that you can compensate for a poor drive or a dubbed iron shot. It is here that tournaments are won or lost.

I have won—and lost—thousands of dollars in prize money within the scoring zone. One year I had a 5-stroke lead in the Los Angeles Open going into the final five holes. A terrific storm broke and I watched four strokes of my lead vanish on the next four holes.

On the seventy-second and final hole I needed a four to win. My drive was good, but my second shot, an iron, hooked when I lost my footing. I was just off the green, in a trap, needing to sink my ball in two. I took out my sand iron, the club that had saved me dozens of strokes in competition. But this time it failed. It dug into the goo and the ball jumped a few feet—that was all.

That stroke cost me the title. I chipped out the next shot and sank my putt, but that was only good enough for a tie and I lost the play-off to Vic Ghezzi.

Then there was the St. Paul Open in which I shot a 65 in the final round to make it a three-way tie with Ky Laffoon and Harry Cooper. In the resulting play-off, the break came on the sixteenth hole of the afternoon round. We all drove well on the par-4, 422-yard hole. On the second shot Laffoon was short and in the rough; Cooper was on the green; and I was long, on the fringe beyond the green.

Laffoon chipped up twenty-five feet from the pin; Cooper putted five feet short of the cup. I chipped my ball and landed three feet from the hole. The next shot told the story. Laffoon putted a few feet past the cup; Cooper's shot was short. Mine went right in the cup. And that was that. They never caught me, although Laffoon missed a heartbreaking fifteen-foot putt on the eighteenth that stopped just a blade of grass away from the cup. If it had gone in, it would have tied us. But it didn't.

It is that way in practically every tournament. The runner-up misses a putt or dubs an approach shot. Sometimes the winner plays such unerring golf that nobody can catch him, but usually it is the story of the also-ran who failed somewhere inside the scoring zone.

And ordinarily it is the missed shot inside the scoring zone that ruins the score of the average golfer.

There are seven places where the average player loses shots:
1. Poor drives.
2. Dubbed fairway shots.
3. A poor shot from the rough.
4. An inaccurate, or flubbed, approach shot.
5. A bad shot from a sand trap.
6. A poor chip shot.
7. A bad putt.

Notice that four of these danger spots—the approach, sand shot, chip, and putt—lie within the scoring zone.

You can make a lot of mistakes in golf and still play a good game if you can overcome the danger spots within the scoring zone. The year I won the P.G.A. championship I drew Walter Hagen in the opening round. He played fine, consistent golf. Meanwhile

I was in sand traps on eleven of the eighteen holes. Yet on every one I came out of the trap so close to the cup that I needed only one putt to sink the ball—and I won the match and eventually the title.

That feat has become a sort of legend in professional golf circles, but plenty of others have won big tournaments in that fashion. As a matter of fact, the pros have a term for that kind of golfer. They call him a "scrambler." He is a golfer who is always in trouble, but who manages to get out. A duffer is a golfer who is always in trouble but who seldom gets out.

He doesn't get out of trouble and his score is never good because he misses shots in the scoring zone. He putts poorly, he messes up his sand shots, he chips badly, and his approaches are haphazard.

Most important of these faults is poor putting. A poor putt wipes out the effect of a brilliant 250-yard drive. A shot lost on the fairway can be made up, but a shot lost on the green is lost forever. It is here on the putting green, in the very heart of the scoring zone, that golf scores are made.

What was your score the last time out? How many greens did you three-putt? What would your score have been if you had dropped the ball in the cup on every green in two putts? Those extra putts make a big difference in your game.

Par for a course is figured on the distance from tee to green and then two strokes are added for putting. A par-3 hole is one up to 250 yards; par 4, up to 450 yards; par 5, from 450 to 600 yards; and par 6, over 600 yards. The distances for women's par are slightly less. Par 3 for a woman golfer is a hole up to 210 yards; par 4 is up to 400 yards; par 5, to 575 yards; and over 575 yards is a par 6.

"Par," according to the United States Golf Association rules, "means perfect play without flukes and under ordinary weather conditions *always allowing two strokes on each putting green.*"

What does this mean in terms of your score? In the previous chapter we figured out *your* par. You can use those extra strokes on the fairways and still break 100—if you sink your ball in two putts.

Therefore it is obvious that the first step in breaking 100 lies in better putting. In earlier chapters you have familiarized yourself with each of the clubs. Now you must work to perfect your game with each of them. Don't overlook any of them; learn to use them all.

But give first priority to your putter and then to the short irons within the scoring zone. They are the shots that you are most likely to miss, the strokes that most likely are keeping your score high.

And now, to understand golf better, let's study a little of the theory of the game.

16 THE PERFECT GOLF SWING

THE OTHER DAY I came across an old yellowed newspaper clipping that quoted from the *American Medical Journal* of 1928. "Golf," it said, "is what letter carrying, ditch digging and carpet beating would be if those three tasks had to be performed on the same hot afternoon by gentlemen who require a different implement for every mood.

"Each implement has a specific purpose and ultimately some golfers get to know what that purpose is. They are the exceptions."

This humorous definition is unfortunately true for many golfers. All too few do know exactly what happens when their club strikes the ball. Until you understand some of the mechanics involved, you will have trouble leaving the beginner's class.

In the early days of golf every club was made by an artisan and each was a little different. Today, manufacturers have standardized their clubs so that each club of a particular model is just like the next. In addition they have spent a lot of money in research to design clubs to fit the needs of today's golfers.

The club is designed to do your work for you.

Let me repeat that. The club is designed to do your work for you. A sand iron is designed to get a ball out of sand traps. Your job is simply to swing the club so that the club face hits under the ball; the club does the rest.

Let us now look at the various clubs to see what each can do. We will learn the whys and wherefores of a good shot and the reasons behind a poor shot.

Each club has a different hitting surface, different because each club has a different function. The main difference is the amount of angle on the club face. A driver is practically straight up and down. Its function is to carry the ball as far down the fairway as possible.

The other woods are designed to play the ball off the grass and are built with more slant to the face to get the ball into the air. The irons have more and more angle to the club face as the number increases. The No. 1 iron is practically straight up and down; the sand iron, on the other end of the scale, is slanted way back.

The more slanted the club face the less distance the ball will travel in the air, the higher into the air it will go, and the less distance the ball will travel after it lands.

With the short irons great slant results in a high lob shot to the green. This is the system used by Bobby Locke, the South African, and by most British golfers.

American golfers, however, use a lower-flying ball with plenty of backspin. That was the system I taught you earlier in the book. Here is the reason that, even with an angle to the club face, the approach shots with the No. 7 iron travel low.

A golf club, when swung properly, moves in an arc. With the driver the bottom of the arc coincides with the spot where the ball is teed. The ball is literally swept off the tee. With the irons, however, the club is still traveling downward as it hits the ball. The bottom of the arc lies anywhere from a fraction of an inch to an inch or so in front of the ball.

That is the reason you "take turf"—your club cutting into the grass—ahead of the ball on the properly executed shot. This downward hit puts a spin on the ball—a backspin—which helps get the ball into the air and which causes it to "grab" when it finally strikes the ground. The greater the slant the club face has, naturally, the more backspin it will put on the ball.

But there is another factor in the swing that produces backspin. With the driver, your feet are well apart and your club, entering the hitting area, comes in low. As your feet come closer together and the length of the club shaft gets shorter, the arc of your swing will be sharper. Thus with the sand iron on a chip shot, your feet are very close together and your club shaft is shorter. The result is a small, sharp arc to your swing.

Let's take another look at the clubs. Pick up your driver and place it so the bottom of the club head is flat on the carpet. Now place a golf ball on the floor squarely in the middle of the hitting surface of the club. Now do the same with your fairway woods and each of your irons, finally ending up with your putter.

This is the exact position at which each of the clubs should strike the golf ball when you swing properly.

Notice, too, another point which Ralph Guldahl, twice National Open champ, made at a recent golf clinic—how large the golf ball looms against the club face. Not much room for error.

One common golf error is to have the club tilted back, thus robbing the club of part of its hitting surface. This also increases the possibility of striking the ball with the heel of the club, resulting in a wild shot.

Now, while you have a golf ball out, take a look at it. Notice that it is covered with tiny holes—or dimples. Their function is to catch the wind and make the ball turn; in a sense they are tiny windmills. They have both a good and a bad function. Their good function is to cause the ball to travel farther and straighter. Scientific tests have shown that perfectly smooth balls travel only about a third as far. The turning motion of a golf ball is similar to the function of rifling in a pistol which causes a bullet to revolve and hence fly straight to the target.

The bad function of those dimples on the golf ball is that an improperly struck ball will spin sideways and curve out into the rough.

As the club is swung, there are three ways in which it can contact the ball. It can strike from straight behind. Or it can hit the ball inward or outward. Let's see what happens in each instance.

Hit from straight behind, squarely in the middle of the hitting surface, the ball will fly straight.

Hit inward toward the left foot, the ball will scrape against the hitting surface and begin to spin. Take your club and rub it against the ball, moving the club toward you. Notice how the ball begins to rotate in a clockwise fashion. This is the same action that results if the club head strikes the ball while traveling inward.

This turning of the ball, magnified by the wind catching in the dimples, causes it to curve in the air. Turning clockwise, it curves clockwise in the air. In other words, it curves off to the right. In golf language, a slice. Notice too that the greater the angle at which the club strikes the ball, the more the spin and, in turn, the greater the slice.

On the other hand, if the club head strikes the ball on an angle outward it will produce a counterclockwise spin and a ball that curves to the left in a hook. Here again, the greater the outward angle, the greater the hook.

The ideal golf swing is one that travels slightly inside-out. This produces a slight hook. It is somewhat better than a perfectly straight ball because it travels a little farther and the turning motion results in a longer roll when the ball lands.

To summarize: the perfect golf swing is one that travels slightly away from the left foot, crossing the line of flight on a slightly outward angle, and in which the club head strikes the ball squarely in the middle of the hitting surface.

Place one of your clubs on the carpet again with a golf ball squarely in the middle of the hitting surface. Now turn the club slightly. This slight turn, if it occurs in a golf swing, will cause the ball to fly off at an angle. In addition it will cause the club to rub along the ball and produce a spin. A club turned outward is said to be "open" and results in a slice. Turned inward it is "hooded" and results in a hook.

This illustrates the reason for the proper grip and for the straight-wrist exercise. Both prevent the club from striking the ball in either an open or hooded position. Let me illustrate another reason for the straight wrists in the hitting area. Place your club behind the ball, using the proper stance. Keep the club head behind the ball but move your hands forward by cocking your wrists. Notice now what has happened to the club face. It is set to drive the ball into the ground. Now move the club back to the right, so the wrists are cocked the other way. The bottom of the club face is now striking the ball. This too would result in a "topped" shot which never gets into the air.

Thus you can see that if your wrists are not straight as the club strikes the ball, your shot will be dubbed. That is why, in my instruction, I have placed so much emphasis on the straight-wrist exercise. It is the only sure way to guarantee that the club face will strike the ball squarely.

And now let's put this golf theory to work in helping to cure your faults.

111

17 CURING YOUR FAULTS

.

MY FRIEND, Herb Graffis, Chicago newspaper columnist, explained his golf swing recently. "I take the club back the way one pro teaches. I keep my wrist firm like another tells me to do. I swing from the inside-out. But when I get the club head to the ball, I become Graffis again and dub the shot."

Herb is doing a little kidding, because actually he shoots a pretty nice game. But there is a lot in what he says.

If you followed exactly the instructions I have given for using the various clubs, there would be no need for this chapter. You wouldn't have any faults. Most times it doesn't work out that way, however.

Why do you have golf faults? The answer is simple. You are not consciously making errors. As a matter of fact, you *believe* you are following the directions implicitly. But—and here lies the reason for golf faults—either you have misconceptions about the game or, more likely, you had some preconceived ideas about golf before you read this book and you haven't freed yourself of their influence.

At least three-fourths of a professional's teaching time is spent trying to straighten out the thinking of his pupil. Trying to help him unlearn some wrong idea he has picked up about golf.

There are three very hazardous thoughts that dwell in the mind of the average beginner. First, wrist action. Second, the

112

pivot. Third, keeping your eye on the ball throughout the entire swing.

I have seen all types of them perform. The wrist flipper. The pivoter. The guy who looks like Danny the Duffer. The three hazardous thoughts are troublesome because each of the actions does occur during a golf swing.

But a golf swing is a spontaneous action of stance, footwork, and hand action. The tempo in a golf swing is "one a-a-and two, swish," the ball is on its way. How many "if's" and "don'ts" can you think of within three seconds? Not many to be sure. That is about the time required from the start of the swing to the moment of impact.

I have talked of hand action earlier in the book. It is no mysterious secret. We are all gifted with a pair of wrists that flex. But the confusion comes in distinguishing between wrist action and hand action. I mean in terms of "feel." If you were pounding a nail or using a sledge hammer, your sense of instinct would re-time the hammer at the split second of impact which forces the wrist to release as nature intended.

Our main objective, therefore, is to make certain we have a good, sound grip that will enable the wrist to cock freely and properly at the top of each swing so that it may also release properly through the hitting area by the added use of the hands.

The second most misconceived thought in the golfer's mind is the pivot. Some actually think a pivot is a matter of picking up the feet like a toe dancer. Others think of doing something with the hips or the body. Remember that a pivot is nothing other than a turn on a fixed axis. By keeping the head in the same position, the body becomes an axis during the golf swing. That is part of the function of my formula. The shoulders must turn and the hips follow, causing a pivot if you follow the formula faithfully. The principal factors in the pivot are stance and weight distribution, with the addition of the quickie rhythm and straight-wrist exercise.

The third item on the golfer's trouble list is the admonition to keep your eye on the ball throughout the entire swing. This is a very overrated statement. Keeping your eye on the ball helps tremendously to hold your body steady and in balance—*until the ball is struck.* But, by all means, let your head and shoulders turn freely at the finish.

Motion pictures prove that the head does not come up to watch the ball in flight until the club head is at least waist high. This gives you an idea of how fast the club head travels.

Don't handicap your game with these three hazardous thoughts, the most common misconceptions of the average golfer.

As in my formula, the important things to feel, by a matter of repetition, are stance and weight distribution, the correct grip, the tempo of the swing, and the right footwork in rebalancing yourself in the downswing.

Balance is an essential to a good golf swing. In earlier chapters I put special stress in starting your golf swing with perfect balance. With a smooth, even swing your movements will flow naturally and you will be in balance throughout the swing.

Good footwork is the secret of balance.

If you have followed the formula carefully, your footwork will be good. In the natural flowing movement of the swing, the left foot turns over on its side during the backswing. On the downswing, it returns to its proper position and then, in the follow-through, the right foot comes up on the ball of the foot.

Here is a good way to check your footwork.

Take your driver and—without stopping—take five full swings.

Keep the club moving steadily from the top of the backswing to the top of the follow-through. Immediately swing it back and repeat your swing.

If you are in balance throughout the swing, this exercise will be a helpful warm-up.

But, if you are out of balance, it will quickly show up. You may be able to swing once or twice, but—if you are out of balance—you can tell immediately. Either you will have to shift your feet or you will have to break the rhythm of your swing. If this happens, check your starting position to see that you are properly balanced. Next, check your left foot at the top of your backswing. Is it turned over on the ball of the foot as it should be?

Finally, check the start of your downswing. Are you *swinging* the club down with the arms, shoulders, and club moving as one unit? Are you controlling the club through the hitting area and

114

letting the club move naturally through its arc in a smooth follow-through?

In the following sections of this chapter, you will find a more detailed explanation of the usual golfing errors in all stages of the golf swing and the major faults experienced by pupils. If you are having troubles, use this chapter as a recheck on your game and follow the simple directions for eliminating your faults.

Putting Errors

The artist in a sketch accompanying this chapter has pictured the most common of putting faults. This golfer has started right with his knees bent, club gripped properly, elbows in, and he is well bent over the ball.

But when he starts to move the putter, he goes all wrong. He lifts the club with his wrists and then slaps at the ball with a snap of his wrists. It would take extraordinary coordination with a lot of luck to make the club face come back square with the ball. It would take an extraordinary touch to gauge the distance properly.

If you are this one-in-a-hundred golfer, maybe you can get away with this putting form. You are, however, giving yourself a tough problem. Oh, you may occasionally drop them in with this putting form, but your luck won't last.

Compare these sketches with the earlier drawings in chapter 4.

Notice that in the correct form the wrists don't give. The putting stroke is accomplished with arms, hands, and club—all moving as one unit. In the wrong form, illustrated here, the stroke is all in the hands and wrists.

The correct form makes it easier to strike the ball with the club face square.

In connection with this point let me suggest a simple exercise that I use with my pupils. Take your proper stance and stroke the ball in the correct fashion. If you are putting for a cup ten feet away, strike the first ball with the club face slightly turned outward. Stroke the second ball with the club face turned slightly inward. Finally, stroke the third ball squarely for the hole.

Notice the spread of the three balls. One hit with an open face, is off to the right, the second with a closed face is to the left, and the last is in the vicinity of the cup. This will be your pattern

115

COMMON ERRORS IN PUTTING
AND STANCE

The top sketches show the wrong putting positions, one of the most frequently encountered errors. Compare them with the sketches earlier in the book showing the correct putting stroke. Properly, the club is swung back with the arms and club moving as one unit. This golfer, however, has taken the club back by bending his wrists. Then he has jabbed at the ball with a flip of his wrists.

Obviously the path of the ball and how far it will go are strictly a gamble for this golfer.

The golfer in the lower right-hand sketch is obviously off balance. The slightest tap on his back would send him sprawling. Yet there is only one major fault. Can you spot it?

It is his knees. They are locked back, instead of being relaxed like the golfer on the left. The locked knees have thrust his weight forward on the balls of his feet, bent him over, and forced him to bend his arms. If the golfer on the right would simply relax his knees, he would straighten up, get his weight back on his heels, and his arms would fall into the correct position.

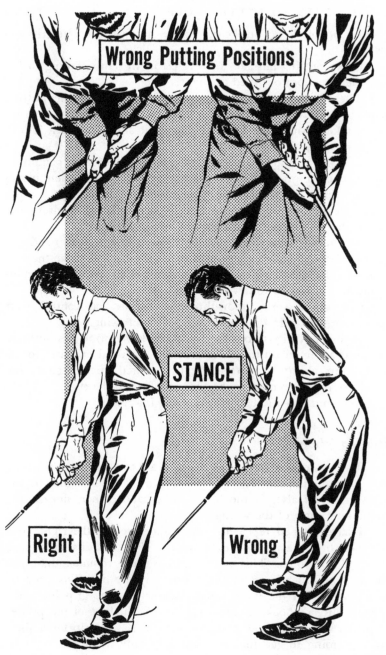

Wrong Putting Positions

STANCE

Right

Wrong

117

of error, if you do not stroke the ball with a firm, accurate grip and swing.

Other putting mistakes involve errors in stance, failing to follow the directions outlined in chapter 4.

There is another common misunderstanding about the putting stroke. This involves the follow-through. Many golfers, erroneously, take a backswing for a ten-foot putt and then use a follow-through of a thirty-foot putt.

A good putting swing is a matter of balance. A pendulum moves back a given distance in one direction and then moves through an identical distance in the other direction. Your putting stroke should follow that principle. Your follow-through should be roughly for the same distance as your backswing.

The importance of the follow-through is simply to rebalance your backswing, and it guarantees that the club will strike the ball properly. Exaggerating the follow-through destroys its effectiveness as much as using no follow-through at all.

Controlling your follow-through, just as you control your backswing, will help develop a firm grip and swing.

If your putting is not effective, recheck the principles outlined in the chapter on putting. Practice the suggested exercises to develop your ability to putt along the desired line. Restudy the step-by-step process of selecting the right line to the cup.

And practice—the best cure for putting faults.

Starting Wrong

The two easiest ways to dub a shot are to grip the club wrong and to stand improperly. The sketches in chapter 5 showed the right grip and also, in the lower right hand corner, showed the commonest form of the wrong grip.

I have stressed repeatedly the importance of the right grip. The sketch of the wrong grip shows the obvious faults; make sure they are not yours. This wrong grip is more common than you think. The other forms of the wrong grip are best illustrated by sketches later in the book where I show you the grip for a deliberate slice or hook. Comparing these with those of the proper grip will show you other common errors. If you grip for a slice, you are going to get one; use that grip only when you want to slice. Or if you are a chronic hooker, experiment with this slice grip to help straighten your shots.

The right stance means good balance, an essential to a good swing. The wrong stance is poor balance, and that leads to a poor swing. On page 117 you will find sketches of the right and wrong way to address a ball.

Notice these features about the wrong stance. The golfer's knees are not bent; they are locked tight. He is bent way over. What do you suppose would happen if you gave this golfer a slight push on the back? Right. He'd fall forward on his face.

On the other hand, note the right stance. The knees are bent; the golfer is standing comfortably. His balance is perfect; he is well set for a good swing.

You can be off balance in four ways. You can be off balance, as in the sketch, with the result that you are in danger of falling on your face. You can be off balance in the other way, that you are in danger of falling backward. You can be off balance sideways. The next set of sketches, showing wrong swings, contains one picture in the lower left-hand corner of a golfer leaning back to the right. A golfer can also be off balance, leaning too far to the left.

In the proper stance you are perfectly in balance. Your weight is back on your heels, balanced by the forward bend at the waist. In the proper stance, your weight is evenly balanced between your right and left feet—giving you balance from either side.

Poor balance is a very common fault, particularly among women golfers. Study the right stance and follow it.

The Rocking Swing

In the perfect golf swing, everything is balanced. The left hand at the top of the backswing is in the same relative position as the other hand, the right, will be at the opposite end of the swing (the top of the follow-through).

This balancing factor applies equally to wrong swings. Starting wrong means finishing wrong.

The illustrations at the top of the page on wrong swings show the rocking swing. This golfer has leaned way ahead of the ball at the top of his backswing. At the end of his backswing he is way back the other way.

FIVE WRONG SWINGS

Upper left. The "reverse pivot." This golfer is doing things in reverse. Instead of lifting his left heel, he raises his right. He has started off balance and is now off balance. His weight is not evenly divided, but over on his left foot.

Upper right. This shows the inevitable result of the reverse pivot. He's still turned around. His left heel, instead of his right, is now off the ground. He has fallen back on his follow-through. His club head has taken a terrific loop en route and when he hit the ball his shoulders were turned open. The result: a bad slice.

Middle. Overpivoting. He is off balance because he has pivoted too far by taking his left foot up on the toe and turning it outward. This is a very common fault among women golfers. When this golfer swings, his shoulders will turn faster than his feet can rebalance. This causes a looping, roundhouse swing— and a bad slice.

Lower left. This golfer is intent on scooping the ball into the air. He is leaning way to the right, off balance. His weight isn't evenly balanced and he can't swing naturally. He'll dub the ball.

Lower right. This golfer is all tied up because he is trying to keep his eye on the ball. His neck muscles are badly strained. He is uncomfortable. There is tension in every muscle. The freedom of a free swing is gone. This fault will take the zip out of a golfer's swing and prevent him from a fast, controlled swing.
COMPARE THESE POSES WITH THE EARLIER, CORRECT POSITIONS.

The golfer with the rocking swing will end his follow-through leaning so far back that he is in danger of falling down. Occasionally you see a golfer with this form who actually does a little jig to keep his balance on his follow-through.

It is apparent from looking at the sketches that nobody knows —including the golfer—where the ball is going to go. The sketch also shows the left arm bent to add to his golfing woes.

The Pivoter

The golfer appearing in the middle sketch on the page of wrong swings has heard about pivots. A normal pivot may be good enough for other folks, but he's really going to do it. This is a common error among golfers who have heard about the upright swing and are determined to get their club shaft down below the horizontal.

Notice the faults. His left arm is bent. His right elbow, instead of pointing downward, is sticking out to the rear. His left foot is up on the tip of the toe and turned outward. This has caused him to turn too far at the shoulders and waist. Also his head has moved way back from its initial position.

If he gets the club back to its starting position, it is strictly luck—because everything is against him. If you are a woman, pay particular attention to the golfer's left foot. That error is most common among women golfers.

This golfer is overpivoting. He should take a shorter swing and let his left foot take the natural movement of moving normally to the ball of the foot with the backswing.

The Leaner

The golfer illustrated in the lower left hand corner of the page is a leaner. As we mentioned earlier, he is off balance. His weight is not evenly balanced, it is all over on his right foot.

A big part of an instructor's job is to try to find out what is going on in the pupil's mind. What is he thinking about to make him commit these errors? A moment ago you met a golfer who was thinking about the pivot and the upright swing.

This golfer is probably concerned about getting the ball into the air.

He thinks he is standing properly.

That is an important thing to realize. Nobody deliberately stands improperly. They are making errors without realizing it. Thus, in checking your own possible errors, you will often need help from another person. The pro at your club is your best spectator; he is trained to pick out flaws. If that isn't possible, a friend can watch you swing and see if you are unconsciously committing one of these errors in swinging.

Our golfer, who is leaning so far away from the ball in his anxiety to get the ball into the air, probably won't succeed. More likely his club will strike the ground behind the ball. And if he hits it, the ball will probably have an erratic flight.

The Watcher

The golfer pictured in the lower right hand-corner has also misunderstood golf instructions. He has been told—and who hasn't? —that you have to keep your eye on the ball. So he is going to continue to watch the spot until long after the ball lands.

He has his eye on the spot, all right, but look at the shape he's in. He is all tied up in knots. This, incidentally, is a very common sight on a golf course.

What are the true facts?

It is true that you should keep your eye on the ball. From the address through the backswing; then down through the downswing and through the hitting area.

As your club passes through the ball and continues on in the follow-through, it still has a long way to go. The turning motion of your shoulders carries the club out and upward on the follow-through. As your club passes your left foot and continues on, you will notice a pulling motion pulling your head up.

Let your head respond to that motion. The continuation of the follow-through will naturally pull your head up to a straight position. This golfer has resisted that natural motion and has destroyed the naturalness of his swing.

As I have said earlier, let nature take its course. Resistance to the natural motions of the swing only means trouble.

It goes without saying, however, that you should not anticipate that motion by looking up until after you are well into your follow-through and you feel the motion pulling your head up. The golfer who peeks too soon is also courting disaster because that pulls his swing out of its arc and results in a topped shot.

The Slicer

By far and away the commonest fault in golf is the slice. Most beginners start with it and are usually recognized by their place on the fairway, diligently hunting for their ball in the rough along the right-hand side of the fairway.

There are two common forms of slice. The simple slice causes a ball to start curving right away, or it goes straight for a little way and then curves. The more complex slice is the pull slice in which the ball starts off to the left and then starts curving to the right.

Let's talk about the simple slice first. As you know from the chapter on the perfect golf swing, there are two ways a ball can be made to slice. One is by an outside-in swing. The second is by striking the ball with an open (slanted-back) club face.

If you have a golf slice, let's turn detective and track down the reason for it.

First, check your grip. This is the most common cause of a slice. Just because I have emphasized the grip often, don't take it for granted that you now have the right grip. If you are slicing, it is a fair bet that, even though you think you are gripping right, you are not.

Do you see at least three knuckles of your left hand as you look down at your grip? If you do not, you are gripping for a slice. The wrong grip means the club face will be open when it strikes the ball. A friend can help you make another check. Swing an iron back to the top of your backswing. Correctly, the club face should be pointing downward at a 45° angle. With the wrong grip, it will be pointing straight, or almost straight down.

If your grip is right, the second logical place to look for the cause of your slice is in your stance. The position of the feet guides the path of the swing. Pulling the left foot back from the line of flight causes the swing to come outside-in with the longer irons

124

and woods. Check that you are standing properly, with the right foot back farther from the line of flight than the left.

The third point to be checked is the golfer's posture. The persons who start off in one of the bad positions I have described before are bound to end up with poor shots. You should be evenly balanced at the start. Any exaggeration will result in errors: if your weight is on one foot; if it is too far forward or too much on your heels; if your knees are not bent; if one is bent and the other isn't. All these things will throw off the balance—and throw you off your game.

There is another posture fault so frequently encountered that professionals often refer to golfers with this error as "natural" slicers. As you know, taking your grip with the right hand pulls your right shoulder lower than your left.

But—and here lies the fault—many beginners also let that right shoulder stick out. Shoulders, hips, and feet should all be parallel at the start of the swing. If that shoulder sticks out, it is going to throw your swing out of line.

The final place to look for the cause of a slice is in the swing itself. It is particularly common in upright, slow swingers.

If you have watched a number of beginners on a driving range, you probably have seen this golfer. He stands right. His grip is right. He swings the club back properly. So far, so good. But, if you watch carefully, the club does not return to the ball on the same plane. It loops. It comes back properly but on the downswing takes an outward loop that throws it into the outside-in path.

Again, as with other swinging faults, it is a question of what is in the golfer's mind.

This golfer is thinking about hitting the ball.

He can't wait for the downswing. He is thinking about it while the club is still on its way back. This golfer doesn't follow the natural swing and the one-and-two rhythm. The tempo goes: Swing it away—hit it!

This golfer doesn't control his club. Often he swings back stiff and slowly and then swings fast on the downswing. His timing is bound to be bad.

In summary, check these four points (in this order): grip, stance, posture, and swing.

The right grip, the proper stance, well-balanced posture, and

WHY YOU SLICE

The top sketch shows slicing at the point of impact. The club is hitting across the ball. The shoulders are open ("pulling away from the ball," in pro language). The club face is open.

The center drawing illustrates the common error of a slice position at the top of the swing. The golfer has not made a complete shoulder turn. He has only half turned, and then completed his backswing by lifting the club—bending his arm and cocking the left wrist underneath.

This causes—as you see in the bottom sketch—the right elbow to point outward and high instead of down toward the right hip pocket as it should.

These sketches show the reasons most golfers slice. COMPARE THESE POSITIONS WITH THE CORRECT POSITIONS ILLUSTRATED EARLIER.

In the top sketch the club should be square, instead of open. The Revolta formula for training your hands to align the club properly is the best cure. A low backswing will help cure the slicer illustrated in the other sketches. Note that the right elbow should be pointing downward. The right hand—not the left— should be under the shaft.

The diagrams at the lower left show the inside-out and outside-in swings. The top diagram of the two shows the inside-out swing, but the club head is cutting across the ball at too great an angle. Combined with an open club face, this will result in a "pushed" shot—one that travels out to the right of your objective. If the club face is square, it will result in a hook. The bottom diagram shows the improper outside-in groove. With a closed club face, it will cut across the ball and produce a slice. The correct groove is a slightly inside-out swing with a square club face, producing a slight hook.

Hook

Slice

the natural one-and-two rhythm swing don't permit a slice. Somewhere along the route you aren't following them.

When I have pupils who slice, I usually follow this routine. I have them take a very closed stance with their right foot well back of their left from the line of flight. This will result in a hook. Hooking the ball in this way helps them understand the factors affecting the flight of the ball.

After they hook consistently from this stance, I have them gradually move their right foot forward toward the proper stance.

I also find that an upright swing normally accompanies these slicers. So I deliberately work to flatten out their swing. To do this I encourage them to scrape their club face along the ground for several feet away from the ball on the backswing. Swinging it away low, with wrists straight, flattens out their swing and helps erase that slice.

If your slice defies detection on your first round of sleuthing, try those exercises of hooking the ball and flattening your swing. It works wonders with chronic slicers.

If you slice, don't surrender to it. Golfers who accept the fact that they slice and deliberately aim to compensate for it just aren't ever going to be good golfers. It is an easy fault to correct if you have expert counsel. And if you give your game a good analysis, you'll have no difficulty spotting your trouble yourself.

Slicing occurs in the game of most beginners. But it isn't natural and a little study will get it out of your golf system.

The Pulled Slice

Quite often the slice is accompanied by a pulled shot. A pulled shot is one that travels out straight to the left of the target. Combined with a slice, it starts to the left and then slices over to the right.

There is only one way that a ball can travel straight out to the left. And that is an outside-in swing. If the club face is straight for that line-of-flight, the ball will go straight out to the left. But if it is square to the correct line of flight, or if it is turned outward, the ball will also slice. Hence, the pulled slice.

In discussing the slice, we stated the primary reasons for the outside-in swing. Swinging the club away low to the ground and with the quickie rhythm cures most pulled shots. Here's why: the flatter swing makes you turn at the shoulders and hips. You can't get the club back with your left arm straight without turning at the shoulders.

The typical pull-slicer turns hardly at all at the shoulders. Standing for an upright swing, he lifts the club up with his hands instead of swinging it back. His shoulders turn maybe a quarter way around, and he makes the rest of his swing with his arms. The arms, in turn, then do most of the work in bringing the club back down—and often, bring it down in the outside-in pattern.

This is the commonest error. Be suspicious of your swing if you are a pull-slicer or simply a pull hitter. Study the sketches of the correct swing that appear in this book. Note how the club starts back low and how it is *swung* back to the top of the back-swing.

There are several checks you can make. Are your stance and posture correct? Are you falling into the errors listed as the five wrong swings? Are your shoulders turned at the top of the back-swing almost to a right angle to the line of flight? Is your right elbow pointing almost straight down? Is your right wrist under the club at the top of the backswing?

Are you swinging the club away—then bringing it down for the "hit it" quickie rhythm?

If your answer is "yes" to all these questions, you won't pull the ball.

The Man Who Hooks

Someone once said that a slice is a blunder; a hook is a good fault. The reason is that a slight hook is desirable. As a matter of fact, beginners are troubled by a slice; professionals are more likely to have trouble with a hook.

Ralph Guldahl says he was troubled by a hook early in his career. In a Canadian tournament he came to the first hole, an easy one where your drive (if you drive as far as Ralph does) almost reached the green. The only hazard was a road along the left fairway. Ralph hit his first over the road. Then his second. And his third. His fourth went into a trap. He exploded into another trap. Eventually he holed his ball for a 9. He had just been married a few weeks and his wife was very proud and hopeful of his chances —before he teed off.

"Right then and there I figured I'd better correct that hook," he said.

Hooking is seldom caused by stance, unless you stand with your right foot pulled back too far. With the correct stance, few golfers will hook badly. The usual cause is in hitting with a closed club face—one turned inward so that it aims the ball off to the left.

As in all golf faults, check your grip first.

More commonly it comes from a failure to have your wrists firm in the hitting area. To overcome this fault was one big reason for my emphasis on firm wrists in the exercise. If your wrists are not straight, they may flop over and the club head will meet the ball wrong.

A failure to swing the club back properly may also end up in a bad hook. A roundhouse swing like a baseball player picking one up from his heels in an effort to clear the fence often causes an exaggerated inside-out swing—and an exaggerated hook.

If your left arm bends, it will tend to roundhouse your swing.

In summary, a hook is a rare ailment among beginners. If, as an advanced player, you develop a pronounced hook, check to see that your grip has not gone wrong. Then, be particularly alert to a failing to control your wrists in the hitting area.

This fault is likely to crop out among golfers who have picked up the idea that uncocking the wrists develops added yardage. They get the mistaken idea that snapping the wrists does the trick. And they snap the wrists too soon and their club face is closed when it meets the ball.

Their timing is off.

It is a common error to become conscious of one factor in the golf swing. Beware of it; it is likely to be sure death on your timing. Go back and spend time on my formula, particularly with a backswing and straight wrists. Then, watch that pronounced hook disappear.

The Pushed Shot

A ball that flies off to the right and then either goes straight or slices is pushed. The club face is open in the pushed shot.

130

Whether, on its flight to the right of the target, it goes straight or slices depends on your swing.

If it goes straight, but off to the right, the trouble is in the position of the club face when it strikes the ball. Your swing has been properly inside-out. But when it combines with an outside-in swing, it results in that terrific slice that ends up a couple of fairways away.

If the bad slice is your trouble, correct the path of your swing first. Then straighten out the club head problem.

We have already discussed the wrong swing, so we'll concern ourselves here with the simple pushed shot—the one that goes straight, but off to the right.

Usually this is an error in the swing. You've seen it already in the sketches of five wrong swings. This was the golfer who swayed to the right on the backswing and then to the left on the downswing. As a result, his body is too far ahead of the ball when the club head finally strikes the ball.

The ball, as you know, should be teed up off the left instep for the long shots. Playing it farther back will also result in the hands and body getting ahead of the ball.

"Staying behind the ball" is a common expression you may hear on the golf course. It means simply that, in the correct swing, the head and most of the body will be in back of the ball at the time of impact.

Pushing the ball may occasionally sneak up on you as you seek to improve your yardage by increasing the tempo of your swing. I have counseled you to swing as rapidly as possible and still *control the club*.

In the correct swing, the body and club are rebalanced to the same position on impact with the ball that they had at the start of the backswing. This must always be true. You can increase your tempo safely only when you can still rebalance properly. Swinging faster without accompanying control will result in pushing.

Check your balance at the start of your backswing. Check that your wrists are straight at impact. Most cases of pushing exist because of errors in those two factors.

High, Low, or Whiff!

Beginners usually start out by missing the ball completely or by scuffing the ground behind the ball. Both are embarrassing, especially to the novice. He has an awe of other golfers, instinctively believing they are all watching his every error and laughing up their sleeves.

Actually, of course, nobody is laughing—mainly because most golfers are in the beginner class themselves or are experienced duffers. They've got nothing to laugh about. Sitting alongside the No. 1 tee at any course for a few hours will show you a constant parade of golfers with errors of one sort or another.

Whiffing is natural for beginners. Their timing is not yet developed. Relatively speaking, they are like the tot taking his first steps—they are bound to fall on their face a few times. Scuffing the ground and topping the ball is the next step for the beginner. His timing is a little better but his coordination is still off.

Scuffing or missing the ball completely rarely happens to a golfer who has experience.

But rather than wait for experience to teach you the causes of your errors, it will help you to correct them now by understanding them.

The fellow who swings and misses usually can do this only by pulling his club up over the ball. This happens because he has pulled up his body; this in turn causes the club head to pull up over the ball.

Commonly this is caused by looking up at the time that your club should be hitting the ball. The head is the anchor for the swing, as you know, and raising this base of your swing will ruin it. The correct stance is formed by bending forward at the waist.

Straightening up the body also will ruin the path of the proper swing.

The third basic reason for missing the ball is that your arms—particularly your left—are bent. The theory of the golf swing—bringing the club head back to the place from which it started—is based on the straight left arm guiding the club. If the arm is bent anywhere in the backswing or in the downswing to the point where the club head strikes the ball, the club head may miss the ball.

If this is your fault, the chances are that you have skipped rapidly through the book instead of studying it and working with the lessons. My best advice is to go back and reread and study the book page by page.

Hitting the ground behind the ball can usually be traced to three faults.

1. Tilting backward on your backswing. By tilting too far to the right, you throw yourself off balance and the club head is actually hitting at a nonexistent ball several inches in back of the actual golf ball.

2. Starting with your weight on your right leg. This means that your weight starts on your right side and ends there. Actually it should be evenly distributed. Results are the same as No. 1.

3. Hitting too soon. The results are the same as above, but the reason is different. In the correct swing the wrists are straight when the club head strikes the ball. If they "hit" too soon, the wrists will already have passed through the hitting zone by the time the club actually strikes the ball. They will have swung right, except for one thing: the ball wasn't where they aimed.

The remedy lies in spending time on the chapters devoted to getting started right and the Revolta exercise. Proper balance and straight wrists in the hitting area guarantee against scuffed shots.

Fairly rare among golf errors are the shots that go too low or too high. Few of you who read this book should have these troubles. I included them simply because of those few thus afflicted and for the benefit of all of you who may sometime encounter them.

A shot that travels too low results from the club face's striking the ball without its normal loft. The club face has been turned over on its face so that the angle is lost.

The usual reason is that the wrists are not straight when they strike the ball—they are still bent back.

The ball that goes a mile high but only a hundred or so yards forward from the tee is an occasionally encountered fault. The wrong swing can result in either a high flier, or a topped shot. It occurs when the player hacks down at the ball instead of swings the club.

If the club strikes the ball in the middle of the club face, the ball will go into the air. If it hits too far forward on the ball, the shot will be dubbed. On tee shots, particularly, the ball is swept

133

off the tee in the proper swing. The too-high or too-low shot isn't. If your club head moves away from the ball in the proper "swing it away" style, neither of these problems need concern you.

There is one other reason for scuffing the ground in back of the ball which is worthy of mention because women golfers often have trouble with it. Remember the golfer earlier in this chapter who overpivoted? His left foot turned way out of line. In another form, the left knee dips.

Both faults push the weight way over on the right leg and when the golfer starts his downswing he ends up by striking the ball with his weight—not evenly balanced as it should be—but still way over on his right leg.

One common reason for it, again, is mental. The golfer knows his right shoulder should be lower than his left. But this should be natural, since his right hand does lie lower on the club shaft. However, he doesn't follow the natural course. He pushes his right shoulder farther down without a reason for it, and sets off a chain of golf errors.

Shanking

As you know from the chapter on the perfect golf swing, the club face should strike the ball squarely. If the toe (front end) of the club face strikes the ball, or if it hits up at the neck (where the club face joins the shaft), it is bound to result in an erratic flight.

A lot has been made of this fault, called shanking, because so many things can cause it.

And so they can. But we won't bother going into them. Simply, it means that you haven't properly judged the arc of your swing or that you have altered your swing en route. Swinging naturally will avert this fault. Usually it is a wrong idea in your golf thinking that causes it to appear.

For example, if you consciously reach for the ball, you will be stretching beyond your normal swing. Then, when you swing right, the ball will lie outside the arc of your swing and you'll hit with the toe of the club.

Rather than trace through a dozen causes of this erratic behavior—you'll notice it if your ball takes a peculiar course and your club will show marks on the neck or toe—simply go back and practice the formula for a half hour, starting with short backswings and gradually extending the backswing. This is the quickest, and easiest, way to halt this unusual golfing error.

Summary

Golfing errors come from two sources: (1) failing to follow the instructions for swinging properly; (2) the wrong mental attitude, either by misunderstanding the instructions or by getting your mind cluttered up with golfing details.

It is especially important to avoid curing one golf fault at the expense of causing two others. Many a golfer, curing a slice, has ended up with exaggerating the cure, and in the exaggeration sending his ball off erratically.

Don't forget my advice early in the book: the easiest way to cure golf faults is not to make them in the first place. If you read the early chapters of this book with an open mind and follow the advice carefully you won't develop errors.

But, if you do develop faults, don't take the cures blindly. Understand what caused them and why the remedy works. Unless you follow the process through completely, you will effect the cure in a half-understanding way and leave yourself a ready victim to other golf errors.

Good golf isn't tough. The golfer makes it so by thinking it is tough. Know what makes a good shot good. You'll then know what makes a bad shot bad. And golfing errors will be neither so likely nor so difficult to cure once you discover them.

18 TIPS FOR WOMEN GOLFERS

IN 1567 political enemies said they had seen Mary Stuart, Queen of Scots, knocking a golf ball around near Seton Castle in Scotland. The gossips said that she was indifferent to her husband's recent death. The story may or may not be true. But it did establish her as the first woman golfer in history.

Today, of course, thousands of women play golf. And they take a great interest in learning to play well.

I have taught hundreds of women to play good golf. One woman from the East Coast stopped off at my club on her way to a Denver tournament for lessons. Ordinarily I don't believe in instruction at that time because it may unsettle the player's regular game. But I did finally spend a few days polishing up a few features of her swing and she knocked off enough strokes to qualify in the meet. Shortly afterward, she won three local tournaments in the East.

There should be no difference in the way a woman swings a golf club and the way a man does. The fundamentals of the swing are the same for everyone. Both men and women are susceptible to the same golfing errors.

However, I have found that the golfing faults of most women fit a pattern. If you are a woman golfer, you will do well to study these typical faults to see if they apply to your game.

The greatest error that women golfers make is in their posture as they address the ball. Invariably they lean forward with their weight on the balls of their feet. Whether this is caused by their natural posture from wearing high heels, I do not know. I only know I encounter this fault with most of my women pupils.

With these pupils I spend a good deal of time teaching them how to stand properly. I explained the right stance in detail in chapter 6, "Getting Started Right." If you are a woman golfer, you will find it profitable now to go back and reread those pages. The improper balance sets off a whole chain of errors in the swing that unduly handicaps many women golfers.

Get the right feel for standing properly. Bend at the knees to give you the feeling of "sitting down" to the ball. When your weight is properly back on your heels, you can feel that weight in the back of your legs.

Practice the proper stance without a golf club; then, standing with the golf club as you address the ball. Finally, be alert to the proper balance as you swing the club.

It is natural for many golfers to forget these fundamentals as they get ready to hit a ball on a golf course. Only by paying particular attention to them during practice can you cultivate the habit of doing the right thing naturally.

Another common fault among women golfers is a tendency to move their head a lot during their backswing. This stems largely from their being off balance to start with. Since they are wobbly on their feet, they strive to keep their balance by moving their head. Getting the proper solid foundation to their stance will usually clear up this fault promptly.

In every shot, the head should stay relatively in the same spot throughout the swing. Naturally, it will turn on the follow-through, but it should not move from side to side, nor up and down.

The side-to-side movement results usually in a woman's moving her head to the left as she swings the club back and then to the right as she swings down. In the previous chapter on golf faults you have seen this fault illustrated and noted the results.

The up-and-down movement comes from errors in the swing.

Most women golfers, particularly as beginners, overswing. This fault is particularly noticeable in the left foot. As you know, in the full swing a good player rolls over on the inside ball of the left foot.

But a woman golfer is likely to go up on the toe of this foot and then turn the foot outward. This is overpivoting. This fault comes from a lack of balance and from taking too long a backswing. It often causes a second fault, that of dipping the left knee instead of letting it shift naturally during the swing.

Taking too long a backswing, I believe, comes from a misconception of the golf swing. Women attempt to compensate for their lack of muscular power by lengthening their swing to get more distance. Actually distance comes from a combination of factors—of which timing is the most important.

Good timing is possible only when the golf club—at all times during the swing—is under control. It can't be under control when you are off balance or when you permit errors in your swing to take the club head out of its grooved path.

In addition to a tendency to turn the left foot outward, many women try to lengthen their swing by bending their left arm at the top of the swing. Now some golfers do break their arm at the elbow at the top of the backswing, but they have to make a *second* error in the downswing in order to bring the club back to its right position in striking the ball.

The reason for having the left arm straight is that it is the simplest way to keep the club under control. This arm guides the club throughout the backswing and downswing and, if kept straight, makes it easier to guide the club head in its proper path.

There is still another fault of many women golfers in their effort to lengthen their backswing. They are very likely to loosen their grip on the club at the top of the backswing in order to let the club drop farther.

The answer to these problems is simple.

Women golfers should not take a long backswing.

They should never take a backswing that allows the club shaft to drop below the horizontal.

How can a woman golfer gain control over her swing and groove her swing properly?

Most women swing the club back too slowly. They have a tendency to move the club back slowly and deliberately—instead of swinging it back. For this reason they should concentrate on the fundamental of the quickie rhythm.

Primarily, I believe women should practice their balance—weight back on their heels and evenly distributed between the two feet. Most other faults are developed from poor balance.

Next, they should spend plenty of time with the straight-wrist exercise. Most women have weaker wrists than men and they must spend time in developing control over the club in the hitting area. They should also develop a flatter swing by starting the club head back in a low path from the ball. A flat swing will make over-swinging virtually impossible. It also compels a good pivot of the shoulders and hips.

A woman's weight and strength don't equal a man's. Therefore her swing will be slower. But it should still be as fast as she can make it and still keep control over the club. Straight wrists in the hitting area and a flatter backswing will enable her to swing faster *with control.*

Another common fault among women is a tendency to scoop for sand shots and for the short iron shots. She is likely to hack down at the ball. This comes from a fear that she isn't going to get the ball into the air if she swings naturally at it and a tendency to try to flip the ball with a snap of the wrists.

Both of these are bad faults which I have discussed earlier in the book. The truth is that the ball will go into the air if you swing right. A wrist flip is a particularly bad fault because it breeds so many other golf errors. It is another strong argument for spending time on my formula with practice in keeping the wrists straight in the hitting area.

In summary, I have found that women golfers must spend more time in practicing fundamentals. Ordinarily, because they are less athletic than men it takes them a little longer to coordinate. None of these faults is very difficult to correct. It simply takes an awareness that they exist and then the patience to learn the proper basic points of the game.

These faults are less dramatic than the long booming slice of some men golfers—but they are just as disastrous on the course. In learning to overcome them, women will avoid the greater, and more stubborn, faults that men develop in their game.

In the long run they will find their progress speeded up—and they will be on their way to easier and better golf.

19 HINTS TO YOUNGSTERS

NEARLY ALL the great golfers started playing the game when they were somewhere between the ages of eight and twelve. They literally grew up with golf. As a consequence, as adults they were years ahead of those who took up the game later on.

I strongly advise all parents to encourage their children to play. It is not only a healthful sport, but it has many long-range advantages over other games. It is an important social asset in these days when more and more people are taking up the game. Playing well by starting young will give the youngster greater advantages in later life.

Also it is a game which can be played for a lifetime. Unlike many other sports that are more strenuous, golf will always be within our physical capabilities.

This has been especially proved, I believe, in our war veterans' rehabilitation centers. Servicemen have regained their health through hours in the sunlight and fresh air. No other sport can be so beneficial, and yet offer so much enjoyment as golf.

The golf profession has taken special interest in youngsters. There is the P.G.A. program for junior golf and the outstanding work of the Chicago District Golf Association.

Recent statistics show that more and more youngsters are taking up the game each year.

Golf clubs who used to prohibit youngsters from playing unless accompanied by an adult are now permitting them to use the course without restriction at least once a week.

Along with many other pros, I am encouraging youngsters to play by giving group lessons to the caddies at our club. No other lessons give me so much enjoyment because I know I am helping to build the future generation of golfers.

I have a young son who started playing when he was very small. I bought him a set of specially made short clubs to start with and he has gradually grown into the longer clubs.

Manufacturers of golf equipment now make junior-sized clubs, so it is no longer necessary to have junior use an old discarded set of your clubs. As with all golfers, it is most important that youngsters have a properly fitted set of clubs so that in their early playing days they can become well founded in their game.

With my son—and other pros follow the same idea with their kids—I let him play his own game. The only time I intrude is when I notice him developing a bad fault.

I encourage him to watch all the great golfers and take him along whenever possible to tournaments. I like to see youngsters experiment. It is only in this way that they can build their own game.

I have advised adults not to try to imitate the great golfers, pointing out that their upright swing is not normally suited to their muscles. But this is not true for youngsters. Their muscles are pliable. Their game can be molded.

For that reason I encourage my son, and other youngsters, to study the actions of all the experts. Experiment. Mimic the actions of all good golfers. Try out their game. See if it suits you.

Experiment with the open stance, square and close stance. Note what happens to the flight of the ball as you shift your feet. Try the short and full swings. Test each phase of the game. Be alert to their effect.

In this way you will be developing a fuller knowledge of what is involved in a golf swing.

But above all learn to control your shots. Pick out the spot where you expect the ball to land. Try to improve your accuracy until you learn not only to control your club but to control the flight of the ball. This is the mark of a truly great golfer.

Youngsters, ten to eighteen years old, often try to hit the ball too hard. Control is far more important. As youngsters grow, their muscles will develop and they will gain yardage. But nothing except practice and improved golf knowledge will ever gain them the ability to control the ball.

It is important for a golfer to know what makes a good shot go right—and especially important to know what makes a shot go wrong. Every golfer, no matter how good he is, at some time will develop faults and his game will go sour. If he has the ability to analyze these faults and correct them, he can get straightened out in a hurry.

I have noticed with pride that my son has gradually developed this judgment. At first he was very impatient and tended to get upset when he made a mistake. Now he is far more patient and has learned to understand his own game better.

Both parents and youngsters must develop patience. Adults are often impatient with the efforts of their children to pick up the game. On the other hand, most youngsters resent advice and revolt against helpful suggestions.

Both are wrong.

Unless you are an expert player, you should hesitate before advising others on their game. A professional is the best man to consult if you feel that the youngster is falling into bad golf habits.

Youngsters often have a "know it all" attitude. Obviously it takes years to develop a complete knowledge of the game—and even then you don't know it all. Every professional is constantly learning more and more about the game.

One of the best ways for a youngster to improve and expand his knowledge of golf is to caddy. It gives him a chance to test his judgment of distance and choice of clubs. It gives him an opportunity to watch golfers of all abilities play and to note the reasons for both good and bad golf.

If your son wants to caddy, however, let him work at some club other than the one to which you belong. The reasons, I think, are obvious.

One of the big troubles that young golfers encounter is lack of coordination. This, as for all golfers, simply takes time and practice to perfect. The fundamentals of my formula are a sound way to develop proper timing and coordination. The straight-wrist exercise is especially helpful.

All youngsters have a golden opportunity to become expert players. A good golf swing, once learned, is not forgotten. Learned as a youngster, it will repay itself many times over in later years.

20 PLAYING A BAD LIE

IF EVERY GOLF SHOT were played on a flat surface, the game would be immeasurably easier. But it doesn't work out that way. A large percentage of your shots will be made with the ball on an uphill or downhill slope or with the ball higher or lower than your feet.

Since the golf swing you have developed thus far is designed for a flat surface, it simply won't work for bad lies. Not without some alterations.

The first requirement for playing from a bad lie is the ability to play the normal shot. Until you have your regular swing grooved and the club under control, you can't be expected to handle these shots. After you have developed consistency in your swing, tackle these tougher shots.

As you know, the right golf swing is an arc from the top of the backswing to the finish of the follow-through. Obviously when the ball is uphill or downhill from your feet, it will not lie in the normal arc of your swing.

When you have to stand unevenly on a slope, the ground is going to interfere with the normal arc of your swing. It will also force you to break the cardinal rule of having your weight equally divided between both feet.

So we have to make alterations in the arc of your swing to handle these shots.

The first thought that must be in your mind in playing bad lies

143

is just that. They are bad. They are a handicap to your game. You can't play them as well as a shot off level ground. So don't try to. You are going to lose some distance. This is important to know and to make part of your golf understanding.

Too many golfers, confronted by a bad lie, don't appreciate the fact. They attempt to hit the ball just as far as a normal shot—and they can't do it. Rather, they should accept the fact that the ball isn't going so far, and concern themselves primarily with hitting the ball straight toward the green.

Let's take up each of the bad lies and discuss the way to play them.

The Uphill Lie

In this shot the ball lies on an upward slope in the direction of the green. When you take your normal stance your left foot is higher than your right. This throws your weight onto your right foot instead of its being equally divided.

This balance is likely to cause you to hook the ball or to pull it to the left because it interferes with the normal transfer of weight during the downswing.

To overcome this tendency play the hook by aiming to the right of where you want the ball to land. Don't forget the principle of bending your knees. But try to balance your weight by trying to keep your weight more on your left foot. This will tend to balance the weight thrown on your right foot by the slope of the ground.

Also, shorten your swing. You don't have so good balance now as you had on level ground and your control isn't so good. By shortening your swing you have less pivot and less of a swing to control—and you can do a better job of it.

Since the ball is lying on an upward slope, it will be easy to get it in the air if you hit it squarely. To keep from losing distance by wasting the power of your shot in a high flying ball, take a club with less slant. This is called "underclubbing." From an uphill lie, a No. 5 iron shot will take the same path that a No. 6 iron shot would off level ground, because the slope of the ground will add that extra loft.

So from an uphill lie always take a club with one less number than you would ordinarily use for that distance.

In summary: A normal swing from an uphill lie will produce a ball that flies too high in the air and which hooks to the left. To overcome this problem, do the opposite. Take a shorter swing, aim to the right, and use a straighter faced club to keep the ball low.

A Downhill Lie

This is a tougher shot. With a normal swing you are likely to either fail to get the ball in the air at all, or to slice it off to the right. In this shot, the weight is too much on the left foot. The club is likely to bump into the ground on the backswing. There is a tendency to chop down at the ball.

All of which means trouble.

Again the answer is to shorten your swing, so that you can control it better. You will also find it helpful to take a slightly wider stance than usual and to stand slightly straighter. The net effect is a more upright swing which causes a sharper angle to the arc of the swing.

Because the normal swing will cause the ball to slice to the right, aim to the *left* of where you want the ball to go. Balance is especially important. There is great tendency to pull up on these shots, and that means a topped shot. Stay down to the ball during the downswing and through the hitting area.

The downward slope is likely to cause the ball to fly too low. For this reason use a club one number *more* than the one you would ordinarily use. Thus, use a No. 3 iron instead of a No. 2.

Summary: Since a normal shot played on a downhill lie will fly too low and will slice, use a more slanted club and aim to the left of your target. Avoid chopping at the ball and raising up in the hitting area. Take a shorter swing, more upright, and then swing naturally.

With the Ball Below Your Feet

This is one of the most awkward shots in golf. The ball seems a long distance away and there is a tendency to reach for the ball and to get your weight so far forward that you are in danger of falling on your face.

A normal swing is likely to slice from this position.

The answer lies in taking as long a hold on the club as possible, gripping it close to the end. Bend your knees a little more than normal and keep your weight back on your heels.

Many golfers find it helpful to play the ball from nearer the middle of the stance than normal. Aim a little to the left to overcome the natural slice. It is especially important to keep down to the ball throughout the swing to guard against a tendency to rise up and top the ball.

Summary: Since the ball is farther away than normal, take a longer grip on the club. Overcome a tendency to fall forward by bending the knees a little more than usual, and keep the weight back on your heels. Overcome the slice by aiming slightly to the left of your target.

With the Ball Higher Than Your Feet

Here the problem is the opposite. Now your tendency is to fall back and away from the ball. The remedy is to concentrate your weight more on the balls of your feet. The ball is closer to you than normal, so shorten your grip on the club.

Use a shorter backswing. The ball, if hit normally, would tend to hook. So aim a little to the right to overcome the hook. Open your stance a little by pulling the left foot back slightly. Many players find it helpful to play the ball more off the right foot than the normal position of playing it off the left.

Again, you have to be especially alert to the danger of rising up in the hitting area. Keep down to the ball.

Summary: The ball is closer to you, so shorten your grip. Shorten your swing for better control. Keep your weight more on the balls of your feet and aim to the right to overcome the natural hook.

Review

You are going to encounter bad lies in playing golf. They are bad because they interfere with your normal swing and you have to alter your regular game. Know the bad effects of these lies, and then it will be easier to remember what to do about them.

When the ball lies uphill or above your feet, it tends to hook. When it is downhill or below your feet, it tends to slice. In all instances, aim your shot to take these tendencies into consideration.

Each of the four cases of bad lies has an effect on your balance. Compensate for this natural factor, by doing the opposite. Where your stance in a bad lie throws your weight forward, overcome this by concentrating your weight on your heels, and so on. In each case, wherever possible, seek the perfect balance—weight slightly back on the heels and evenly balanced between the feet.

In most cases shorten your swing to gain better control over it. This is particularly important in uphill and downhill lies.

In uphill and downhill lies, remember that they affect the flight of the ball. An uphill lie will cause the ball to go into the air, a downhill lie will cause it to fly low. In these cases don't use your normal club. To overcome the height of an uphill shot, use a straighter-faced club. To get the ball into the air from a downhill lie, use a more lofted club.

In all cases, make your adjustments and *then* swing naturally. Remember to keep down to the ball, because there will be a natural tendency to lift up during the swing.

Bad lies are the best test of your golf and the timing of your swing. Licking these shots will definitely show up in an improved game with your normal shots. When you have learned to play these tough ones, you can consider yourself well on the way toward becoming an expert.

FOUR BAD LIES

In the upper left-hand sketch, the ball is lying on an upward slope toward the green. The ball is played from its normal position off the left instep. The left knee is bent a little more than normally to balance your weight properly. Aim to the right of the objective to overcome a natural tendency to hook.

Just the reverse happens in the upper right-hand sketch where the ball is on a downward slope. The ball is played more off the right foot and the right knee is bent more than normally. In swinging the club, keep it low on the follow-through. Let it stay with the contour of the slope.

In an uphill lie use a straighter-faced club than usual; in a downhill lie, a more lofted club.

In the lower left-hand sketch, the ball lies higher than the feet. Take a slightly open stance with the ball off the right foot more than usual. The club is gripped farther down the shaft because the ball is close to you. This position tends to hook the ball, so aim slightly to the right.

In the opposite position, where the ball is lower than the feet, the club is gripped as near the top as possible. You stand closer to the ball with a square stance and play the ball off the middle of the stance. The knees are both bent more than normally to bring you down to the ball. The width of the stance is normal. In the lower right-hand sketch the feet are closer together because the golfer is making a very short shot. For a longer shot, they would, of course, be farther apart.

21 FOR THE EXPERT: A DELIBERATE SLICE

IN HIS EARLY DAYS, Frank Stranahan, one of the best amateur golfers in the country, didn't know how deliberately to slice or hook a ball. That was one of the valuable pointers which Ben Hogan gave him when Frank came to him for lessons.

As a matter of fact there are few average golfers who know how. Most of them hook or slice, but not on purpose. Often a golfer who usually slices comes to a spot where a slice would help him and, for once, his slice leaves him and he hits it straight.

At least once in every round you will encounter a situation where a hook or slice is helpful. Shooting around corners on dog legs is a common situation. On many holes a tall, thick tree lies between you and the green. It would be very valuable to know how to curve the ball around that obstacle.

As you know from the chapter on the perfect golf swing, there are two ways to make a ball slice. One is by hitting from the outside-in so the club face scrapes along the ball, giving it a spinning motion. The second is by making the club face strike the ball in an open position—that is, laid back on an angle instead of striking the ball squarely.

The easiest way to produce an outside-in swing is to stand with an open stance, your left foot pulled back. The easiest way to open up your club face is to change the grip of your hands on the club.

The muscles of your arms cause your hands normally to fall slightly cupped. In swinging your arms, the muscles will ordinarily cause your hands to fall in a particular position. The right grip, as I explained in chapter 5, takes advantage of this fact. So when you grip the club properly, the normal action of your arms and hands will bring the club face down squarely to meet the ball. In the right grip, as you know, the "V's" of the thumbs and forefingers are pointed to the right shoulder.

Shift your hands farther around to the left, so that the "V's" are pointing up at your chin. Now, when your hands come down in their natural fashion the club face is going to be turned so that it is on an angle aiming out to the right. That will give you the open face to produce a deliberate slice.

So, to produce a deliberate slice open your stance and open the club face. Pull your left foot back and shift your grip to the left. The combination will result in a shot that curves to the right in a slice.

Hitting a deliberate slice is not only valuable when you need that sort of shot, but it is also helpful in understanding the elements behind a slice, when it is not deliberate.

And now for its counterpart—the deliberate hook.

22 FOR THE EXPERT: HOOKING ON PURPOSE

Hooking on purpose involves doing the opposite from deliberately slicing. It requires a definitely inside-out swing and a closed club face.

To hook a ball, take a more closed stance with the right foot drawn back farther from the line of flight. A closed club face is one in which the club face is at an angle pointing to the left of your target. Striking the ball from this angle causes it to turn counterclockwise and hook.

Producing a closed club face is done in the opposite fashion from opening it. To produce a slice we shifted our hands to the left, so the "V's" were pointing upward. To close the club face you should shift your hands to the right of the normal position.

In both shots—deliberately slicing or hooking—the answer lies solely in changing your grip and the position of your feet. Nothing else.

Having taken your altered grip and stance, then just swing naturally. The changes in your hands and feet will do the rest.

23 FOR THE EXPERT: THE WAGGLE

PERHAPS you are wondering why I have not mentioned the waggle earlier, and why now it is included in the instructions for the expert golfer. The truth is that I almost left this chapter out—on purpose.

I hesitated because I have found the waggle the hardest lesson to teach golfers. Not one pupil in a hundred learns to waggle his club properly. For most golfers the waggle, poorly done, is of no help. In fact, it can be downright detrimental.

The waggle, as you know, is the preliminary loosening up motions with the club before swinging.

But it is also something more. And here is where most pupils go wrong. It is a preview of the tempo of your full swing—something like a drill sergeant counting cadence a few times before he orders his troops to forward march. It is, moreover, a test of the proper hand action to make sure that you have the right feel in the hitting area. And, finally, the good golfer uses the waggle to check the path of his swing to make sure he is aiming for the right spot on the fairway.

Except for the pros and top amateurs, most golfers wiggle the club a few times under the impression that they are doing a waggle. They are just wasting their time.

There are some so-called waggles that are definitely harmful. You have probably seen this kind of golfer. He takes his stance.

153

THE HOOK AND THE WAGGLE

The bottom sketch shows the grip for an intentional hook. Both "V's" are pointing well over at the right shoulder. The right hand is well under the shaft. From eye level you can see all knuckles of the left hand. Combined with a quite closed stance, this will produce a deliberate hook.

As you swing the club with this stance and grip, your normal muscular reactions will cause the club face to be closed at the point of impact and will normally result in your right hand turning over the top of the left as shown in the upper sketch.

The golfer who hooks—but not on purpose—can usually trace his trouble to the upper sketch. His hands have turned over at the point of impact, closing the club face instead of letting it hit the ball squarely.

The diagrams at the right show the waggle used by most good golfers. On the count of one the club is raised a short ways. On the count of two it is swung back. On the count of three it is swung down just above and behind the ball. On the "pause" it is dropped to the ground in back of the ball. It is one continuous, rhythmic motion of "one, two, three, pause."

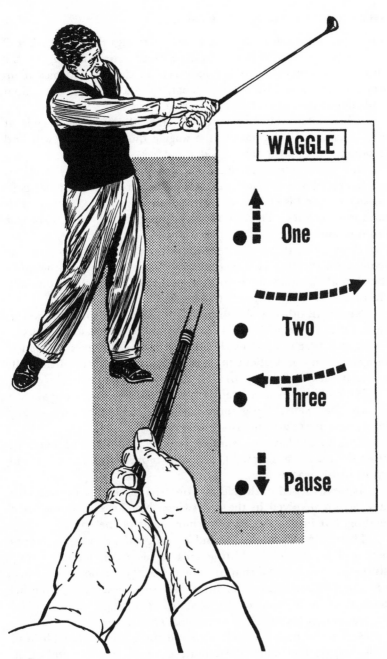

WAGGLE

One

Two

Three

Pause

Then, moving nothing but his wrists, he swings the club back and forth a few times. Nothing could be worse. He is *picking up* the club in his waggle and it is almost certain that he will pick it up when he starts his backswing. That, as you know, is a cardinal fault in golf and almost certain to result in a slice.

This golfer would be better off if he didn't try to waggle at all. In fact, until you master the waggle thoroughly, you will find it doing more harm than good.

It is not an out-and-out essential to good golf. Jimmy Demaret, the fellow who wears the most colorful outfits in professional golf, doesn't waggle his club at all. He simply steps up to the ball with both feet together. Then he moves his right foot over to its proper position and swings.

Henry Picard has the very slightest of waggles. He takes his stance with the club behind the ball. Then, fairly slowly, he raises the club about four or five inches and replaces it behind the ball. He repeats this three times; then swings.

Nearly all other professional and top amateur golfers, however, have a definite waggle. Their waggles are of two definite types.

One is best typified by Tommy Armour. He takes his stance, swings the club back about three feet; returns it in back of the ball; swings it back again; returns it to the ball and pauses.

His club moves in a steady rhythm. One—two—three—pause.

On the "pause" he glances down the fairway and makes any adjustment necessary in his stance.

This waggle has some similarity to my formula. *But* Tommy's wrists do not remain straight. There is movement. There is *hand action* in his waggle.

As we discussed in the chapter on driving, there is considerable hand action involved in the full swing. Not loose, flopping wrist bending, but firm and controlled movement of the hands.

There is a crispness, life, and zip in Armour's waggle, just as there will be inside the hitting area as he makes his full swing. His tempo is steady and snappy, a model of the tempo of his swing. It is a perfect preparation for his swing. In a sense he is giving his hands their last-minute instructions before they go to work.

He repeats his waggle three times. Then swings.

Meanwhile he has closely observed the path of the club head in the waggle and made the minute changes in stance indicated.

156

He is coordinating the path of the club with the path he wants it to follow on his full swing. At each pause he has glanced down the fairway to check his judgment.

With three waggles he has had three chances to double-check.

Unless your waggle has those three functions, beware.

The other general type of waggle is equally popular among the pros. It is the one I use myself.

My waggle also has a count of one, two, three, pause.

On the count of one I raise my club up about a foot. On the count of two, I swing it back about three feet. On the count of three I swing it back right behind the ball, but a little way off the ground. On the pause I drop the club in back of the ball. Each motion flows into the other. There is no hesitation. It is a continuous motion of the club head.

I likewise glance down the fairway on the pause and make necessary adjustments in my stance. In all waggles there is no adjustment of stance while the waggle is going on—only during the pause.

Tempo in each form of the waggle is most important. It must be even and steady. One, two, three, pause. One, two, three, pause. One, two, three, pause. SWING IT AWAY—HIT IT!

A good golfer who uses the waggle uses it with every club.

With the driver, of course, the waggle is longest. It is shortest with the short irons.

The reasons are twofold; the shot is shorter and the amount of hand action is less. From the driver down, the distance is less; the hand action is less; the waggle is shorter.

But for all waggles the rhythm is steady, the hand action is controlled, and the path of the club and the spot on the fairway for which you are aiming are observed and minute changes in stance are made. When your waggle meets these requirements, you have reached the one-in-a-hundred class among my pupils.

Until then, better think twice before you employ the waggle. You may be simply waggling yourself into trouble.

But if you get your waggle down pat—then you are moving into the expert class.

So—to waggle or not to waggle is up to you. It will be your toughest test as you act as your own pro.

24 LICKING THE HAZARDS

In the 1948 tournament at Tam O'Shanter Country Club in Chicago, Bobby Locke knocked his tee shot off to the right. Between his ball and the cup was a high tree. He could play the shot safe, but would lose his chance to tie the winner. He had to gamble.

He arched a high lob shot for the green—a shot for which he is famous. It was dropping straight for the cup—but a tree branch was in the way. The ball struck and caromed off, and with it went Locke's chances.

Professionals have to gamble on the course. An extra stroke picked up on a gamble may be the margin of victory. Everything is in their favor. They are playing for a break, but it isn't a hopeless gamble. Even a pro can't take silly chances.

The beginner, however, is always gambling—and generally losing. He throws away anywhere from five to ten strokes a round on poor gambles. He gambles on a few extra yards on his drive. If he wins his gamble he has a No. 6 iron shot for the green instead of a No. 5 iron shot.

Obviously the pay-off, even if he wins his gamble, isn't very important. And if he loses his gamble, he winds up with a poor tee shot, either way short of his usual drive or off in the rough somewhere. He has gambled away one or two shots on a bet that probably won't gain him a single stroke, even if he wins.

That's bad gambling in anybody's book.

Or, take the beginner who is confronted by a water hazard. If he gambles for a few extra yards, he can land on the far side. If he plays safe, his ball will land just this side of the hazard.

Again, if he wins he is only a few yards closer to the green—but still an iron shot away. If he plays it safe, he is an iron shot away. So he gains little, even if he wins. And if he loses, his ball drops into the water; it costs him a penalty stroke; and then, when he drops the ball, he is just about where he would have been had he played it safe.

Again, this is a poor gamble. Yet a surprising number of beginners take that kind of gamble regularly.

There is still another spot where the beginner makes a poor gamble. That occurs when he gets into trouble. He lands in the heavy rough. The gambler takes a No. 2 iron and swings. Even if he gets a good shot, it won't have anywhere near normal yardage. But more likely he won't be so lucky. Generally he will hit a dubbed shot and he is still in the rough.

If, on the other hand, he plays it safe by pitching the ball out onto the fairway he then has a clean shot for distance. At worst, this safety play will cost you a stroke. Playing it the other way will usually cost you two or more strokes.

You can take this as a good rule: when you land in trouble on the golf course, your first concern is to get out. If you can pick up yardage, all well and good. But first get out of trouble and out on the fairway where you belong.

The next time you play, avoid gambling against the odds. You will be surprised how many strokes you can pick up that heretofore you have thrown away.

From the very bad lies, use your sand iron. Its weight and design will carry it through the thick stuff and toss your ball out onto the fairway. Where the rough isn't quite that bad but still plenty thick, use a No. 7, 8, or 9 iron and play it like an approach shot.

Sometimes you can use even a No. 5 or 6 iron. But in your selection consider the loft needed to clear the hazard. The tall grass gets between the club face and the ball and muffles the shot. So if you are undecided between two clubs, pick the one with the greater loft and play it safe.

In this—and all shots involving hazards—there will be a strong inclination to swing harder than normally. Picking the right club and swinging it naturally will get you out of the rough. Trying harder will only cause tension—and a dubbed shot that doesn't get you out.

Sand traps you already know about.

We have also discussed the usual forms of bad lies. There is another bad lie that you may occasionally encounter, although it is fairly rare. That is the close lie, as a rut in which your ball falls. Obviously you cannot make the normal swing because its arc won't fit down to the ball. The answer here is an upright swing with a lofted club. As you know, this results in a sharper arc to the swing and will get the club face down to the ball.

Another minor problem is dandelions, heavy clover, and other types of thick growth on the fairway. Occasionally your ball will land in that stuff and it may prevent the club face from striking the ball cleanly. In this case use a slightly more lofted club than usual.

A very important hazard is trees. In previous chapters we discussed how deliberately to hook and slice a ball to get around hazards. But there will be times when you want to shoot either over the trees or under their branches.

To make a relatively short shot, but one which travels unusually high in the air, you will, of course, use a very lofted club. It will be an approach shot with a No. 7, 8 or 9 iron or a sand iron. To put more height on this shot, do two things. For one, play the ball more off your left foot. Second, hit the ball with more of a sweeping motion. To do this, swing the club away low, as you do in a drive. As your club returns in the downswing, it will come in at a low arc and sweep the ball off the ground. This sweeping motion and placing of the ball farther forward will enable you to make full use of the club loft and get it high in the air.

More often you will find yourself in a spot where you have to go under the tree branches. Your ball has landed a short way from a tree so you can't go around, and you are too close to go over the top.

For this shot you need a low-flying ball. A normal shot would rise and strike the branches and drop dead. My favorite club for this shot is the No. 4 iron. Then I play the ball farther back toward my right foot.

There is also a helpful little trick that you may want to add to your game. That is "hooding" the club face, already mentioned.

This is done by moving the hands farther forward than the mally are. Try it out yourself. Drop a ball and place your iron in back of it with your normal stance. Now shift your a little to the left. Notice what happens to the club face. I tilts forward, taking away some of its loft.

By hooding a No. 4 iron you turn it into a No. 3 iron. plus playing the ball farther to the right, will result in a low-f ball, but with still enough distance to carry it to the green.

Finally, of course, there are water hazards. Sometimes a river or creek, sometimes a lake, or occasionally a pond. S seaside courses involve holes in which you shoot across an i On these hazards, there is nothing I can tell you. There are tricks to playing them. No fancy shots.

This hazard is entirely in your mind.

With many golfers you could put the smallest pond in fron the tee and they'd be sure to dub their ball into it. Obviou the trouble is all in the mind.

A common water hole has water right in front of the tee. H far is it to the other side? Usually anywhere from ten to possi a hundred yards. Why shouldn't the simplest shot clear t obstacle? It would—except Danny the Duffer is afraid it won't.

Sometimes the water lies along the edge of the fairway. W does Danny always hook or slice into it? Again, it is because is afraid he will.

Failure to clear a simple water hazard in front of the t comes from an uncertainty about your game. Just as many playe spoil their shots out of sand traps by trying to lift the ball, so man try to lift the ball over the water. This usually takes the forr of raising the club head within the hitting area and results in topped ball that plops into the water.

The answer, of course, is that any normal shot will clear th water hazard easily. When you are firmly convinced of this, watei hazards will no longer be anything more than interesting scenery Concentrating on hitting the ball, once you've lined up your angle to the green, is the best way to mask out the hazard. After you've licked that water hazard a few times, you'll gain confidence in your game and never doubt that your shot will clear. And it will.

The reason Danny hooks or slices into water lying alongside the fairways also lies in uncertainty and fear.

Let's see what happens when Danny comes up to a tee with water or some other hazard lying along the right of the fairway. If he slices he will drop in. Danny knows this, so he decides to play it safe. He'll play along the left fairway. So he tees the ball up and gets set to swing so the ball will go to the left. So far, so good.

But let's take a look at his stance compared to the stance he would take if he were going to hit the ball straight. Because he is aiming left, his left foot is back of where it would normally be. But that's an open stance and an open stance produces a slice. And the slice that results from his swing, instead of carrying the ball out of danger, curves it over into the water.

The opposite happens when the hazard is on the left. A ball that is hooked will go into the water. So he tries to play safe by aiming right. He puts his left foot forward. But that makes a stance for a hook, and hook the ball does, right into the water.

On the other hand, had he aimed straight down the fairway and hit it that way, he would never have been close to the water.

Where water cuts across the fairway or lies in front of the green, treat it with respect—but not awe. Play it safe. If you can clear it with a normal shot, go ahead. But if you have to get added yardage to clear, don't gamble. Play it safe by dropping your ball on this side and then take a second shot to clear the water and hit the green.

All the hazards I have outlined in this chapter require only that you use common sense, as long as you know your game—your abilities and your shortcomings. If you know your abilities, it is a simple matter to translate them into proper action as you encounter these golf problems. Knowing your shortcomings, you know when you are unnecessarily gambling by trying to play beyond yourself.

One effect of hazards on a golf course is to make your scoring problem a little tougher by cutting down the distance you would get from a normal shot.

But a more important effect is on your mental outlook. For every shot a hazard costs you mechanically, it will cost you three in wrong thinking. Those shots you can save by thinking right—playing safe, playing smart, and playing confidently.

25 REDUCE THAT SCORE!

IN THE FIRST THIRTEEN CHAPTERS of this book you learned the normal functions of each of your clubs. Subsequently, you learned of the common golf faults, the ones most likely to affect your game, and how to correct them.

You have also learned the harder shots of golf—the unusual problems on a course. And we have discussed the mental side of golf, the ideas that handicap the average player and the poor gambles that cause him to keep his score high.

If you have studied these lessons diligently and tried them out in practice, your score should be dropping.

Regular review of my exercise and quickie rhythm will improve your timing. Poor golfers practice very little. Good golfers spend plenty of time on the practice tee. They spend plenty of time warming up before beginning a golf round.

Many a time I've played a round and found trouble controlling a particular club. After the round I've gone out to spend hours practicing shots with that club until I've licked the problem.

I realize that the average golfer can't spend the time that I can. After all, golf is my business; to you it is a sport. But devote whatever time you can to practice if you want your game to get better.

You can expect your score to get better only when you can handle every club in your bag. You can't expect to play well if you drive extremely well but dub your short shots. Strive always for a well-rounded game.

Generally speaking the poorer golfers are more likely to ignore practicing with their short irons. They are likely to go to a driving range and work on their drives. And they spend time on the practice green to improve their putting.

Don't forget what I have pointed out in earlier chapters. It is in the scoring zone that most golfers miss their shots; and it is in this area that scores are made.

In Chapter 14 I outlined the way to break 100.

If you have successfully passed that hurdle and are consistently shooting in the high 90's, it is time to bring the score down to 90.

Ninety, on most courses, permits you to go one over par on every hole. So adjust your thinking. Take your score card and change the par figures by adding one stroke to each hole.

Let's see what that means in terms of the yardage on the average golf course. In showing you how to break 100, I put special emphasis on the necessity for sinking the ball in two putts. In my experience, good putting is the quickest way to break the century mark.

To bring your score down to 90, you must perfect your short game. You have to sink the ball consistently in three shots from inside the scoring zone. Your putting has to be good. Then you have to gain accuracy in chipping the ball to the cup, blasting out of sand traps to the pin, and hitting the green on our approach shots.

You can take your extra stroke in getting to the scoring zone.

The longest par-3 hole is 250 yards. Your aim should be to get on the green in two shots. Two putts will bring you in in four, which is your par.

If you get on the green in one shot, and sink your ball in two putts, for a par, so much the better. But let your first consideration be to get on the green in two. Play safely to two, rather than gamble to hit the green in one.

On par-4 holes, aim to hit the scoring zone (up to a hundred yards from the green) in two shots. If your second lands close to the green, so much the better. It will simplify your short game. But set your sights to get inside the scoring zone in two; let any additional yardage simply be profit.

On par-5 holes, aim to hit the scoring zone in three shots. Aim for the scoring zone, instead of the green on your third shot.

Once inside the scoring zone, set your goal to sink the ball in three shots.

If you can meet these goals, you will be shooting 90.

Following the same general principles that I laid down in the chapter on breaking 100, take your extra stroke right from the first tee. If you pick up a stroke by shooting par, add that immediately to the par for the next hole. If you fail and go over your par, forget it. You will possibly pick it up later.

Above all, play it safe. Even where you know you will go over your par, take your licking on that hole. Consistent golf will, in the long run, be your best guarantee of shooting lower scores. Gambling to pick up strokes still has no part in your game because the odds are still against you.

Fill out score card 8 on the back end leaves to help you set your sights.

In figuring your par, add one stroke to the card's par. In figuring yardage, deduct 100 yards (that is, the scoring zone) to give you the yardage needed to get to the scoring zone. Your fairway score is the number of strokes you took to reach the scoring zone.

Par in the scoring zone I have set at 3 for every hole. For your score inside the scoring zone, mark down the number of shots you take once you get inside the 100-yard mark.

In keeping a record of the score card you will easily note the phase of your game that needs improvement. If your score in the scoring zone goes over your par of 3, it means you'd better spend time on your putting and short game.

If you are hitting the mark of 3 strokes inside the scoring zone, but still not getting down to 90, analyze your drives and shots with the fairway woods and longer irons. Chances are that you will find one club that is giving you trouble. The obvious answer is to devote practice time to polishing up your game with that club.

Also be alert to fairway shots that you are throwing away through bad judgment or bad gambles.

Par-3 holes give you your best chance to pick up bonus strokes by shooting par. If you can hit the green on your first shot and putt well, you will be in the cup in par. That is one stroke you can use to make up for errors on other holes.

When you have broken 100 consistently and then reduced your score to 90, you are well on your way to the expert class.

26 TIPS FOR BAD-WEATHER GOLF

THE FIRST SUGGESTION, and the most important, for playing in bad weather is to get off the course when a lightning storm strikes. A tragic number of golfers have been killed or injured because they stayed on the fairways when a lightning storm came up.

Under these conditions, seek shelter in a building if possible— the bigger the better.

Avoid, however, small sheds and shelters if they are in an exposed place. Also avoid isolated trees, wire fences, high places, and wide open spaces. Lightning is more likely to strike there.

If you can't get to a safe building, seek shelter in a deep valley or a cave.

But in all events at the first hint of lightning, discontinue play and seek shelter. After the storm resume play where you stopped.

Other types of bad weather in which you may find yourself while playing are rain, after-rain heavy turf, and high winds.

In the 1941 San Francisco Open, a match-play tournament, I went into the final round with Harry Cooper. Much of the match was played in pouring rain and the course was water soaked. There was a miniature lake on one fairway and the greens were covered with water.

Putting conditions were so bad that on ten greens I used a No. 9 iron and chipped, instead of putting and five times it went in! I had sixteen one-putt greens by the thirtieth hole and I was four under par. The match ended there 7 and 6.

The important thing to appreciate is that you cannot play your best golf in bad weather. Many players seek to speed up their swing to overcome the handicap of bad playing conditions and they succeed only in magnifying the problem.

Actually you should play more cautiously in bad weather. Your score, at best, is likely to be several over your normal game. Better settle for that instead of gambling and running up a bad score.

Wet turf makes unsure footing. In each shot make sure your feet are firmly set by digging in with your spikes. In rain, your hands and grip are likely to get slippery, so wipe them off before taking your stance.

Concentrate on hitting the ball straight. The rough is even rougher in wet weather. Keep out if you can.

In bad weather your first interest everywhere on the course should be to get the ball into the air. Therefore make a special effort to hit the ball cleanly. In the rough take a more lofted club than usual.

On the fairway you will not get normal distance from your shots. The heavy going will take most of the roll out of your shots. So you will often find it advisable to use a club with less loft—for example, a No. 3 iron where you would normally use a No. 4.

Since wet greens will slow down your putts, take this into consideration while estimating your distance to the cup.

Wind has surprisingly little effect on a well-hit, straight ball. But if you have a slice or hook it will be exaggerated by the wind.

Many golfers have the same bad habit of playing in wind that I described in the chapter on licking the hazards. If they have a cross wind, they try to hook or slice the ball into the wind to counteract its effect. Too often they end up by simply exaggerating the hook or slice.

In wind, play your best golf and seek to keep the ball straight down the fairway. Often you will find it helpful to take a shorter backswing than usual to gain greater control over the ball.

On a particularly windy day, you may improve your game by playing the ball lower than normally. A low-flying ball, having more speed, is less susceptible to influence by the wind.

167

As you know, a club with less loft will result in a shot with less height. In selecting your club for a particular shot keep that thought in mind. In chapter 24, in describing how to shoot a golf ball under tree branches, I described a way to produce a low-flying ball.

This shot will take practice before you achieve the proper timing. Well executed, your club face returns to the ball in the same hooded position from which it started.

Spend a little time practicing for bad weather. Then when it comes you will be well prepared for it.

Wind makes seashore courses normally a shot or two tougher than inland links. If your course is subject to stiff winds, you will have to take more time working on these shots. The overseas courses, of course, are the toughest for wind. When Bobby Jones won the British Open at St. Andrews there was one hole where he used a No. 8 iron in the morning and a No. 2 wood in the afternoon. Playing under those conditions calls for masterful golf.

27 HOW TO PRACTICE

PRACTICE makes perfect is an old saying and it certainly applies to golf. If you are alert to your golf game, you learn something every time you swing a golf club. Every shot, to the smart golf pupil, adds to his store of knowledge.

You can learn plenty by playing. But a football team doesn't try out a new play at Saturday's game. They have spent their practice sessions perfecting their game before they meet their opponent.

On the course, if you make a poor drive on the first tee you have to wait until the next tee to try again. You simply don't have time to work out the answers to your golf problems.

The solution, of course, lies in the practice tee. There you can test out a single club as long as you want, practicing until you have it down letter perfect. These days there are practice driving ranges in most cities. If there is one near you, take advantage of its opportunities. It is particularly helpful to week-end golfers who have little time during the work week to practice.

A practice range ought to be just that—a place to practice. Too many golfers tee up one ball after another figuring that every now and then they'll get away a good shot. On the golf course, you don't have that chance. Your first shot has to be right. So use your practice time that way. Study each shot—in practice or on the course—and play it the best you can.

169

But in practice, if you make a bad shot you have ample opportunity to note your error and to correct it. That is, if you use your practice time and facilities properly.

There is a great tendency, particularly at driving ranges, to practice only driving. While it is the most dramatic shot and very important, good driving alone will never make a good golfer. Use your practice time to develop a well-rounded game by working with all your clubs.

I have stressed throughout this book the value of good putting. It is indispensable to good golf. It can be learned only with plenty of practice. Every course has a practice putting green and you will find it profitable to work out there whenever you can find time.

And don't forget, in your practice time, to spend time on the other shots—hitting out of sand traps, hitting an intentional slice or hook, hitting a deliberate low shot or unusually high one.

One theory of training airplane pilots was to simply give them ground instruction in parachute jumping. Why practice what you have to do right the first time? was the idea. The opposing view was that a man often had to jump from a plane in distress and if he had jumped in practice he would be better able to handle himself in an emergency.

I believe in the theory that golfers should practice the shots that they may be called upon to make only occasionally. If you have practiced the tough shots, they won't be tough when you need them in the regular course of play.

In addition, I believe practicing the unusual shots gives you a better understanding of how to play the easier ones. Knowing how to hook a ball, for instance, will help you cure a hook if it develops in your regular shots.

Particularly important is your practice time before playing a round. Baseball players have their infield practice; football players warm up before a game. So should golfers.

As in all sports, your first concern is to loosen up. To do this, take a few full swings with a wood club. This will warm up your arm muscles and loosen up that waistline.

After you have warmed up your muscles, start with your putter and test out your timing and judgment on the putting green. Give yourself plenty of time here.

170

In each shot be alert to your own movements and the results. After each shot ask yourself: Where did the ball go? Why?

Start out with the short one-foot putts. When you have sunk them consistently, move back a foot. Gradually move back until you are trying the long twenty-footers. This is the best way to sharpen your putting touch.

After you have finished there, start working your way through the clubs. Start with the sand iron, then the No. 9, 8, 7, 6, 5, 4, 3, 2 irons, then the No. 4 wood, No. 3 wood, and driver. If any of the clubs don't feel right, take time out to go through the formula, first with the short backswing and straight wrists and then gradually extending your swing.

Finally try a few more putts. Then, as you step up to make your first drive, take a few practice swings.

Most golfers do not take time out to get warmed up before they start.

Perhaps it sounds to you like quite a ritual. But actually you will find that a half hour will cover this warm-up period adequately. If you are doubtful about its results, try it out for a couple of rounds. Most golfers find it saves them several strokes, particularly on the first few holes.

There is another form of practice that you will find helpful. If you can't get out to the practice tee, you may find a little free time around home. Why not get out in the backyard and swing your clubs. You can't hit a regular golf ball there, but there are cotton practice balls that you can. Or, you can simply swing a golf club.

The backyard is an ideal place to practice my formula. It will train your muscles for the right feel to the proper swing—the greatest lesson in golf.

And then, you can practice indoors—but I'll wait and tell you about that in the next chapter.

28 WINTER CONDITIONING

MOST GOLFERS put their golf clubs away in the fall and take them out in the spring. While a few hardy souls play even when there is snow on the ground, nearly every golfer gives up until the weather gets warm.

The few exceptions are those lucky enough to live in a climate that permits year-round play or those who can afford a winter vacation.

But if you are conscientiously interested in improving your game, you can keep up your practice during the winter and let it pay off in the spring—by practicing in your living room.

There are a number of golf exercises that can be done indoors. They are very valuable—more valuable to the winter practicer, perhaps, because in regular golf weather he is likely to be too impatient to work on them.

Your living room rug makes a fine practice putting green. Judging the right line to the cup is something that comes to most golfers only with practice. Why not place a water glass on its side and practice trying to put golf balls into it with your putter?

In chapter 4 I outlined another valuable putting aid: putting with a piece of wood. If you strike it squarely, it will move along in a straight line. If it isn't struck right, it will move off line.

You can also get valuable practice time on the straight-wrist exercise. There is no chance of knocking over lamps with this swing over a limited area. In this book I have stressed the importance of training the hands to function properly in the hitting zone. Wintertime gives a wonderful opportunity to concentrate on this vital lesson.

The straight-wrist exercise, employing your full bag of clubs, will help develop your wrists and a sound, firm grip. The proper hand action in the hitting area is the single most important step in the proper golf swing. If you spend time on it during the winter you will be months ahead of your opponents who store their clubs when the snow flies.

If your ceiling is high enough, you may also be able to practice a full swing with some of your clubs.

Using cotton practice balls with the sofa for a backstop, you can spend plenty of time working on your chip shots. Timing and hand action are the secrets of good chipping. That's exactly what you will be learning in your winter practice work.

If your wife protests that your practice is hurting the rugs, get a piece of old carpeting and put it down over the regular rug and hit the practice balls from there.

In many cities there are indoor practice ranges and golf schools that give you another outlet for your winter practicing.

Take time out to reread this book too. Everything you need to know in order to play excellent golf is included within its covers. Going back and reading it again not only will be a good review, but in rechecking you may find pointers that you overlooked the first time through.

If you spend a little time each week in winter conditioning your golf game, you will find marked improvement in the spring. You will help keep yourself in trim and not have to waste valuable golf games in getting back into form.

Winter practice may not be very spectacular, but if it means knocking a half dozen strokes from your score—and well it may—it will be time well spent. Don't you agree?

29 PROFESSIONAL SECRETS

RECENTLY I played with a foursome. One of the players said he had gone to every tournament in the vicinity during the past three years. Yet, when he was just a few feet off the green, he took a full swing with his club.

He had been at every tournament. But he hadn't been watching. No pro would have played the shot in that fashion.

If you have the opportunity, attend professional golf tournaments. You will have a chance to see in action the great golfers of the day. A beginner can gain valuable pointers by watching the smooth-flowing swing of the top golfers and by observing the way in which they play each shot.

As your game improves, the tips picked up by watching the pros become increasingly valuable. It is easier to translate their game into terms of your own.

There are no secrets to the game, from a mechanical standpoint, that I have not given you. I have also outlined the other phases of the game.

Now professional golfers play better than you, first, because they have played many more rounds. They have far more experience and training. Their golf judgment is sound.

Their timing is superb. That is what you must constantly be seeking as you develop your own game: coordinating every movement to gain speed in the club head.

Professionals also have full control over their clubs. Sure, they make mistakes. Every golfer does. But they are aware of their mistakes, and what causes them. Seldom does a professional make the same mistake twice in a single round of golf.

The secret of professionals is simply that they put into practice the points that I have outlined in this book.

All that separates you from their class is the ability to put these principles into effect.

That, of course, isn't possible for every golfer. Probably only two or three golfers in a hundred shoot regularly in par and subpar scores. The greatest handicap is lack of practice time.

Occasionally I have pupils with all the time in the world at their disposal. One southwest oil man flew to Chicago one day for a practice lesson in the sand traps. He had an important golf date and wanted to prepare for it. I worked with him for several days and he flew back to win his match.

Many professionals start slipping in the tournament circles when they lack time to compete regularly. They lose their competitive edge and they no longer win top money. Professional golf must be a full-time job. Except in rare cases, top amateur golf must be a full-time job.

There is nothing, however, to keep you from playing good golf, even if you are confined to playing only on week ends. Practice during the week, either at a practice range or in your own backyard, will help you overcome the lack of actual playing time.

In chapter 25 I outlined the steps to reduce your score to 90. That score gave you the leeway of shooting one over par on every hole.

Below 90, your score is going to drop a stroke at a time because progress will be slower. Set your goals to meet this gradual process. Start taking away your extra stroke from the easiest holes. Try for par on those holes. As you succeed, knock them off the other holes in the order of their toughness.

Work on correcting your faults. As you approach par, you can no longer afford bad shots because they keep your score up.

It is advisable to devote time to fundamentals, because they are essentials to accurate shots. Accuracy is at a premium in the 70 and 80 brackets.

But you will find that added yardage is also valuable at this

175

stage of your game. You gain distance by perfect timing and by speeding up the tempo of your swing. Strive gradually to get a faster tempo; not so fast that you lose control over the club and start hitting erratically. This will be a danger at this point of your game.

A careful job of speeding up gradually will not throw your game off.

Working with a professional is always helpful to a golfer, whatever his abilities. As you seek to reduce your score below 90, you will find the assistance of a competent professional a valuable aid. He will be able to point out small, easily overlooked errors in your game that you may miss yourself. He will help you develop a polish to your game.

Analyze your playing, shot by shot. Make a chart for each hole, following the sample below. Fill in the comparison summary at the end. This will give you the equivalent of a playing lesson in which I'd go along with you as you negotiate the course.

I have permitted you six possible strokes per hole, which will allow you one over par on par-5 holes. Naturally on the shorter holes, you will not need the extra spaces, so cross them out. Mark down the number of the club you use on each shot. "F.S." is an abbreviation for fairway shot; note the wood or iron you employ between the drive and the scoring zone. "Short" covers the scoring zone in which you will either approach, chip, or blast from a sand trap.

Under "Comment," make notation on yardage, accuracy, and any other pointers that you would like to review later.

Under the notation "Comment on Hole," list the hazards and other problems in connection with the hole. Mark down any information which will help you review and analyze your game.

For future rounds, you may find it helpful to take along a pocket notebook on which you can keep similar score cards of your round, shot by shot.

Now take plenty of time to analyze your record. There is a reason for every unsuccessful shot. It is up to you to find out what happened. Don't comment simply that "it went wrong"; determine why it went wrong. Until you know the answers, you won't be able to correct your faults.

First let's look at your putting record. How many putts did

Hole: *Par:*   *Yards:*

Shot	*Club*	*Comment*
Drive		
F. S.		
F. S.		
Short		
Putt		
Putt		

Your Score:

Comment on Hole:

Hole

1	2	3	4	5	6	7	8	9	10	11	12	13	14	15	16	17	18

Par:

Your
Score:

Total Score:

you take? Did you miss any five-footers? Were your long putts rolling in close to the cup?

If you expect to play good golf, you cannot miss the short putts. Your long putts must be stopping very close to the cup if you are going to keep your putting score down to two putts a green.

What was your record on chip shots and sand shots? You should always be getting these shots up to the green. But to play good golf you should do more. You have to drop those chip and sand shots up next to the pin for an easy putt.

Were your approach shots hitting the green consistently? Where did your approach shots drop when they failed to hit the green? Were they short? Long? Off to one side? Why?

Check your record in the scoring zone for consistency.

Every now and then even the poorest player will get away a good shot. That's the reason most hole-in-one shots are made, not by the pros, but by average golfers. Harry Gonder, Michigan City, Indiana, pro once hit 1,817 balls on a 136-yard hole vainly trying to get a hole in one. Nearly all his shots hit the green, a number landing in a five foot circle around the cup. But none dropped in.

So check not only the results of your shots in the scoring zone, but check them for consistency. If your shots with a particular club didn't hit a regular pattern, it means that you have not mastered that club and you need more work with it.

What was your record on tee shots using clubs other than the driver? Were you hitting the green with your iron tee shots on the short holes? If not, where were they landing and why?

What was your driving record? Was your distance consistent? Were your drives long enough, or can you get more yardage? Were they accurate, or did you slice or hook some of them?

What was your record with fairway shots? Did you use every club in your bag? It is a rare round in which you will not be called on to use each one. If you find yourself consistently ignoring one club, find out why.

How did your distance record compare with average shots: No. 2 iron, 170 yards; No. 3, 160 yards; No. 4, 150 yards; No. 5, 140 yards; No. 6, 130 yards; No. 7, 120 yards? Were you consistently beating these averages?

In analyzing your game, understand your errors. A slice will show up with wood clubs and the long irons. A slice in the shorter shots will show up as a shot that consistently lands to the right of where you are aiming. It means your club was open at contact with the ball.

A hook in the short shots will show up as a shot that lands to the left of your target—meaning that your club face was closed at contact.

What was your record with the tough shots: bad lies? freak shots (such as shooting under tree branches, etc.)? Did you try any intentional slices or hooks? Did they work?

Now analyze your comments on the individual holes. Which ones gave you trouble? What were their characteristics (sand, rough, water, etc.)? Did these hazards throw your game off?

Did you make any bad gambles? As your game improves and your score goes down, some shots that are gambles to the 100 player are now even-bets or odds-on. Knowing your abilities will help you decide whether a particular shot is a gamble with the odds in your favor or simply a hopeless gamble.

Keep a careful record of your progress. It is the best check on errors that may creep into your game. It is an ideal test of the consistency of your game. The big errors will be apparent; it is the less noticeable ones which gradually sneak in that are the toughest to detect. A shot-by-shot record of your game will help you detect them.

Use this check as a guide to your practice work.

How good a score you shoot is up to you. A close watch on every shot will help you along.

30 PLAYING FOR THE CADDIES

WHILE MANY GOLFERS are content to play the game for the fun of it, many find it more sporting if they have a wager on the outcome. Playing for the caddy fees, drinks at the nineteenth hole, or a friendly wager are particularly common among players who team up regularly.

I remember one time when Claude Harmon and Chris Dumphy, a well-known Florida sportsman, were playing golf at Palm Beach with a foreign nobleman. The pro shop was about twenty-five feet off to one side of the first tee.

The nobleman's drive went off at a weird angle, right through the door of the pro shop.

"I'll bet a hundred dollars to a dollar you can't do that again," Chris said.

"You don't know my husband's golf," said the nobleman's wife. "It's a bet."

The nobleman teed up, waggled a few times, and swung. And the ball went right through the door of the pro shop.

They began to play. Chris had given the visitor a 40-stroke handicap on a $500 bet. As they neared the first green, Chris asked, "How many do you lie?"

"Six," replied the nobleman.

"Are you sure?" Chris persisted. "I believe you have taken eleven strokes."

"Oh, no."

"But what about the ones you missed," Chris continued.

"Oh," said the nobleman. "In my country we don't count the misses."

"Hmmm," Chris mused. "But for our bet you lie eleven."

"All right," said the nobleman. "For you I lie eleven. But for my country and my morale I lie six."

There are two basic ways of scoring golf. One is by strokes and the other by holes. Tournaments that are figured on the basis of total score are called medal play. These are the most common among the professional tournaments. The other form, of which the best example is the P. G. A. or the National Amateurs, is match play. It is figured on the number of holes won. Thus, if you and I are playing match play and you win the first hole, you are 1-up. If I win the second, we are all even.

When one player is more holes up than there are still left to play he wins the match. Thus, if at the end of the sixteenth hole I am three holes ahead, I would be declared the winner 3 and 2 (*three* up and only *two* holes to go).

Most golf club championships are played off by match play.

There is still another form of professional play, of which the International Four-Ball match is the best example. You play by teams. Henry Picard, a truly great player, used to be my partner in these matches. This is also sometimes known as "best" ball. It is simply a variation on match play. The player who wins the hole wins for his team. And the team that wins the most holes in the match is the victor. Henry and I set a record by winning the International five times. Once we won when Henry dropped a 25-foot putt over the worst possible area of the green. It sloped and slanted in every direction, but he had played it perfectly and it had just enough legs (roll) to drop in the cup.

Another form of competition used in tournaments between teams from rival country clubs is team play. The members pair off against members of the other team and each match counts a point. The team winning the most match points takes the team championship. This is often on a Nassau basis.

The "Nassau" is one of the most frequent forms of wagering on golf. It involves a three-part wager: (1) low score on the first nine holes, (2) low score on the second nine, and (3) low score for all eighteen holes. One bet might be a five-dollar Nassau. The low scorer on the first nine holes would win five dollars. Low scorer on the back nine would win five dollars. And the man whose combined score for the eighteen holes was low would win five dollars.

A "Scotch Foursome" is also popular. The foursome divides into two teams. Each hole is a separate wager. Whichever of the four players sinks his ball in the fewest strokes wins one point for his team. Another point is given to the team whose combined score for the hole is lowest. Thus, you and I are teamed against Smith and Brown and we are playing the first hole. I score a 3; you and Smith score 4's, and Brown has a 5. You and I win one point because my score was lowest on the hole. Your score and mine totals 7; Smith and Brown's total is 9. So we win a second point.

Another popular form of play is used when husband-and-wife teams compete or when a foursome consists of two good and two fair players. Each team uses one ball and the players take turns in hitting it.

There is also a variation called "Syndicates" that can be played with three, four, or five players. The player with the low score on each hole collects from everybody.

Another golf wager bears the title: "Bingles, Bangles, Bungles." It is a three-part wager: (1) the first man to get his ball on the green, (2) the man whose shot on the green lands closest to the hole, and (3) the first man to sink his putt. This game, of course, follows regular golf rules in that the man farthest from the hole always shoots first.

A special wager is sometimes used on par-3 holes. This is called "Proxies." The winner is the man whose first shot lands closest to the hole. Since these are short holes, it normally means the man whose shot on the green is closest to the hole.

There is also a rarer form called "Bridge" golf, which is played by teams of two. One team bets that its combined score on the hole will be so much. The other team can either accept the bet, or "bid" that they will make a lower score. If they make their score, or less, they win a point. If they fail, they pay a point. As in bridge, the opponents may double—doubling the bet; and, again as in bridge, the bidders may redouble the bet.

In this form, of course, the team either makes its bid or

doesn't. In the other wagers, however, ties may result. Generally, most players count ties as canceling the wager.

Some golfers however play "Carry-overs." In this, the money from tie bets is kept track of. The first player to win a hole then collects for that hole and for all the previous bets that were carried over because of ties.

A very common wager is that of low score, figuring in handicaps. A player's handicap is figured by taking his usual score for eighteen holes and then subtracting par. The difference is his handicap and that is deducted from the score he makes on a particular round.

To illustrate. Suppose you and I, Smith and Brown are playing a foursome. If I usually shoot par, I have no handicap. Let's say your usual game is 80; Smith 85, and Brown 90. If par is 72, your handicap will be 8 (your usual score of 80, minus par of 72, equals 8). Smith's handicap will be 13 and Brown's 18. After we finish our round, we find that I have scored 70, you have 77, Smith 83, and Brown 88. Then we figure out our "net" score. Mine is 70 minus 0, or a net of 70. Your score is 77 minus your handicap of 8, or a net of 69; Smith's is 83 minus 13, or 70; and Brown's is 88 minus 18, or 70. In the net score Brown, Smith, and I all have 70's and you have a 69, so you win.

Score cards normally have a space marked "handicap" which can be used when you are wagering on each hole. The handicap holes are numbered, starting with the toughest. If your handicap is 8, you are entitled to subtract one stroke on each of the eight toughest holes; Smith's 13 handicap entitles him to deduct a stroke from the 13 hardest holes; and Brown, having an 18 handicap, can deduct a stroke on each hole. And now for some advice on how to win your golf wagers.

31 | HOW TO WIN AT GOLF

IN THE PREVIOUS CHAPTER I have discussed some of the ways that golfers wager on their game. Until you get fairly proficient, I think you will find it unwise to bet. Not because you may lose—although that may be important—but more because some forms of wagering may tend to ruin your game.

If you try too hard on your drive, for instance, in order to win a bet, you may let yourself get into bad golf habits that are hard to break.

The answer to winning your golf bets, of course, is to play good golf.

As you already know, trying too hard, or pressing, will ruin your game.

Horton Smith tells a story that I think best illustrates that point. Two Englishmen were watching a tournament when Harry Vardon, one of the game's greatest players, missed a four-foot putt.

"Humph," snorted one of the spectators. "Why anybody could sink a short putt like that."

"I'll wager 100 pounds that you can't sink that putt," said his companion, "provided I may make one stipulation."

"It's a bet," said the first. "I'll go get my club now."

"Oh, no," his friend said. "That is my stipulation. We will settle the wager one month from today. I don't care how you spend your month. You may practice that putt as many times as you wish. Then, in a month we will settle our wager."

All that month the man practiced the easy four-foot putt. But he was also thinking about his bet for a month.

"He was worrying so when the day of the bet came that he was shaking like a leaf," Horton Smith said. "Naturally he missed the putt."

There are in golf, as in other sports, some men who are so-called "money players." When the chips are down they seem to play even better than normally. My best advice is just not to get mixed up with them, if you can help it.

But the pressure will tell on most players. If you have made a wise bet at the start, you can win if you play your regular game and avoid getting rattled under pressure. Play your own game and don't worry about what your opponent is doing.

If you can put pressure on your opponent, his game will tighten up and he won't play so well as usually.

Start out right by spending time on the practice putting green and then get well limbered up by practicing with your clubs before starting out. Then step up to the first tee and take your normal swing. Strive for a good clean hit, rather than trying to drive the ball a mile.

There is a good reason for getting warmed up and getting your first drive off well. Most golfers of the week-end variety—and that covers the majority—don't warm up. Instead they warm up after they play a few holes. That's the reason most of them shoot better golf on the second nine holes.

You can take advantage of this by warming up in advance and by starting to play good golf right from the first tee.

Now you know what causes pressure on you during a golf game. A bad drive. A dubbed shot. A ball that lands out in the rough. Those same pressures will affect other golfers, your opponent among them.

If you and your opponent both normally play about the same game, the player who keeps his head under pressure will win. So, if you want to win, relax. If one of you is going to tighten up, let it be your opponent.

If your opponent doesn't have that ability to keep cool, he will make errors and you will win his money. Concentrate on playing your own game and playing it well. Let him worry about his game.

There is an advantage in shooting first. If you get a good shot, the average player will try to duplicate it. So if your opponent outdrives you, take advantage of it. You will have the first shot on the fairway. Make it good. He may match you the first time, but sooner or later he'll crack under the pressure.

If, on the other hand, he has the first shot on the fairway, you can turn it to your advantage. Notice the club he uses for his shot and what results he gets. If you both shoot about the same game and he tries a No. 6 iron and is short, you can profit by his mistake in selecting your own club.

Try to sink your putts. If you putt first and drop yours in, the pressure is all on your opponent and pressure is a tough task master on the greens.

That's why so often in tournaments you see or read about a well-known pro missing an easy three- or four-foot putt. When you've got several thousand dollars riding on a putt, the pressure is terrific. Even the easiest putts are torture when the going gets tough.

Now, suppose you are playing good golf, but your opponent is playing even better. There is a great temptation to start gambling with your shots and trying to get added yardage over your normal game. That's like plunging in a poker game to make up your losses. Usually it doesn't work.

If your opponent is "hot," the best thing is just to wait him out. He can't last. Even if he goes through the eighteen holes without cracking, the percentages will catch up with him the next time out and then it will be your turn. Generally, however, he will cool off some time during the round. If you haven't lost your head and started plunging, you will catch up with him then. When his game begins to cool off, he'll start gambling to keep his run going—and then you'll have him.

Keeping cool under pressure is tough. It is easy advice to give, but not always easy to follow. I know; I've felt that pressure plenty of times myself. The best remedy is to concern yourself only with your own game. Play each shot as it comes and think only about playing it as well as you can. Have confidence in your game. Play within your capabilities.

A good professional competitor never hears the gallery. He is concentrating on his shot and he is oblivious to everything else. If you can learn to keep cool under pressure by thinking only about your own game, the other fellow will be buying the drinks at the nineteenth hole.

32 GOLF RULES

In 1917 a finalist in a tournament at Pinehurst chipped a ball that caught in the cuff of a spectator's trousers. There was a hurried conference. Finally the referee announced his decision. "You'll have to play the ball from where it lies," he said.

"Not on your life," protested the spectator. "I'm not going to have a divot taken out of my leg."

The referee stood his ground and the player tried to persuade the reluctant onlooker to stand still so he could play his shot. At last the two went into a huddle and came up with a solution.

The spectator removed his trousers and held them at arm's length as the golfer neatly lofted the ball onto the green. Amidst cheers the spectator replaced his pants and the contestant sank his putt.

Generally speaking, however, the rules for playing golf follow pretty largely the earliest principles laid down by the Scotch originators of the game at St. Andrews: you have to play the ball from where it lands.

It is a pretty good idea to follow the rules, even as a beginner out on the course for the first time. Getting a ball out of the rough by a gentle push of the foot, or scooping the ball out of sand with a surreptitious flip of the hand when nobody is looking may fool everybody. Everybody that is, except yourself. Your game will actually improve only when you meet—and lick—every situation on the course.

In addition, following the rules may have other angles. I know a man who uses a golf course to double-check his own evaluation of salesmen and employees. "You can tell a man's character best on a golf course," he says. Many a man has lost a job, or a contract, playing with that man because of the temptation to overlook a stroke.

Through the years a lot of details have been worked out by the rules committee to answer all the situations that have arisen in the game—too many for the average player to worry about. If you are playing in tournaments, you will want to study the complete rule-book. But, for the usual golfer, here is a handy simplified summary of the rules for informal match play (not tournament competition).

Teeing off. At the first tee, the "honor" of driving first is decided either by agreement or by chance, such as flipping a coin. Thereafter the man winning the preceding hole has the honor. When both players score the same on the preceding hole, the man who held the honor retains it.

You must tee off within a specified area. At each tee are two markers. They are moved periodically on most courses to let the grass grow back. The ball must be teed up within an imaginary rectangle of a depth of two club lengths directly behind the line indicated by the two markers.

Only the ball must be inside this rectangle. You can, if you wish, stand outside the area. If you drive off out of turn or if you tee up outside the specified area, your opponent may force you to drive again. But there is no penalty.

In getting ready to drive, occasionally you may accidentally knock the ball off the tee in addressing it. It can be teed up again without penalty. If, however, you swing at the ball and either miss or hit it, it counts a stroke, even if it moves only a few inches.

Playing the course. Everywhere on the course—on the fairways, in the rough, and on the putting green—the man whose ball lies farthest from the cup shall shoot first.

If you can't find your ball within five minutes after you or your caddie begins to search for it, it shall be considered lost. Another ball shall then be dropped as near as possible to the place from which the lost ball was played, and a penalty stroke added to the score; the original stroke on which the ball was lost is counted in the score. Thus, if your second shot becomes lost, you drop a ball under penalty of one stroke, and your next stroke is your fourth. If the lost ball was played from the tee, the new ball may be re-teed. The foregoing procedure does not apply to a ball lost in a water hazard or in casual water in a hazard.

If you deem your ball unplayable, the same rule applies.

If the ball goes out of bounds, you proceed as in the case of a lost ball except that there is no penalty stroke. Thus, if you go out of bounds on your tee shot, your next stroke from the tee is your second.

When a player, after hitting a ball, believes that it may be either lost or unplayable or out of bounds, he may immediately play another ball, provisionally, to save time. If he then finds his first ball playable in bounds, he shall pick up his second ball and continue playing with the first. If, however, the first ball is lost, unplayable, or out of bounds, he shall continue play with the second ball under the penalties stated above.

A ball shall be played from where it lies, except in these cases, among others:

1. When it lands in so-called "casual" water: puddles from sprinkling, rain, etc. Or when the player must stand in such water in addressing the ball.

2. When it lies against obstructions such as a guidepost, tools, vehicle, bridge, bridge planking, seat, hut, shelter, or similar objects.

3. When the ball lies on, or touches, obstructions such as those above and clothes, ground under repair, drain cover, hydrant, exposed water pipe, or a hole made by the greenkeeper.

4. When the ball lies within two club lengths of these obstructions and they interfere with the golfer's swing or stance.

As you have noticed, none of these is a *normal* hazard on the golf course. For that reason you may move the ball. Here's how to move the ball. The player should stand erect, face the hole and drop the ball behind him over his shoulder. The ball should not come to rest closer to the hole than it was. If it can't be dropped without rolling nearer, it may be placed. If it rolls into a hazard, it may be redropped unless it was lifted from a hazard, in which case it must be replaced in the hazard.

189

When it is possible to move the ball on the putting green, it must be placed no closer to the cup than its original position. This applies when the ball lies in water, or when the player must stand in water to putt.

So-called loose impediments (leaves, loose stones, dung, worm casts—obstructions not fixed or growing) are not hazards and may be moved out of the way.

The player may lift his ball to identify it, but must replace it in the identical spot. In the strict letter of the rules, he must first notify his opponent.

A ball in play may not be cleaned. If it is so damaged as to be unplayable it may be changed after notifying your opponent. Mud sticking to a ball while in play does not make it unplayable. In medal competition, cleaning a ball illegally costs two strokes; in match play it causes loss of the hole.

Also, according to the strict rules, if a player moves some loose natural impediment and it causes the ball to move, it shall cost a stroke. If the player or his caddie causes the ball to move in most other ways, it usually shall count a stroke.

A hazard is any bunker, water, ditch, or sand—except, as we discussed earlier, casual water. If a ball lies or becomes lost in a water hazard or in casual water in a hazard, a new ball may be dropped *behind* the hazard, under penalty of one stroke, so as to keep the spot where the original ball last crossed the hazard margin between you and the hole. If the original ball was played from the tee, the new ball may be teed.

When both balls are on the putting green and one interferes with the other, the one nearer the hole may be lifted only if it lies within six inches of the other ball or within six inches of the cup.

If your putt strikes your opponent's ball, he may replace it or play it from where it rolls. If your shot knocks his into the cup, he shall be considered as sinking his putt without a stroke.

In addition to these rules, many clubs have their own local rules. Usually these are printed on the back of the score card. When you play a strange course, note their special rules before teeing off.

Incidentally, there are a few rules of courtesy in playing that you should note. You should not talk, move, or otherwise distract a player while he is making a stroke. You should not tee up your ball until after the man with the honor has played. A rule of etiquette and safety is that you shouldn't play until the players ahead are safely out of range.

You should avoid delaying the game by moving promptly off the putting green when you are through. While searching for a lost ball, you should wave the following players on through. You should not take an undue amount of time in playing your ball.

You should replace any turf cut up by your stroke and should smooth out any holes made in sand traps. Avoid damaging the putting green with your clubs, bag, or flagstick. Where you have incurred a penalty, you should notify your opponent promptly.

Most courses have rules for determining who has precedence on the course. As a general rule a player playing alone has no standing, and other groups may pass through.

In any cases not covered in this general summary, you should consult the official rules book. Otherwise rely on common sense. If a dispute arises that cannot be settled, refer it to your club's rules committee or to your pro for settlement.

33 A FINAL WORD

In 1941 I was playing in the Western Open at Phoenix, paired with Lloyd Mangrum in the first round. I had made a discouraging showing in four California events and was anxious to get back on my game.

Mangrum started strongly, knocking six strokes off par on the first five holes. But I was content. My game was sound and I was two under par. As we teed off on the sixth we had picked up a fair-sized gallery. My second shot found the left trap guarding the green.

Just as I was ready to try an explosion shot, a voice from across the green thundered out:

"Oh, there's Revolta. I bet you a buck he gets down in two."

The gallery roared as I stepped back from the ball to try to regain my concentration. It was very still when I walked back and dropped my shot next to the cup and putted it in.

Walking to the next tee, a man came up. "Thanks, fellow, you won me a buck," he said.

Mangrum hooked his tee shot on the seventh and I pushed mine into a sand trap.

"Oh, boy, is he in trouble," said a voice. The same voice. My friend.

In trying to get out of the trap, I hit a tree and the ball came down five inches from the trunk. My fourth shot landed in a wagon rut, and—well, I ended up with a 7.

After I holed my ball, my friend walked up. "Think nothing of it," he said in an inspirational tone. "You can take it." And he walked off to help someone else in the tournament.

Needless to say I had to wait for another tournament to get my game back.

There are going to be times that every golfer's game will go bad.

Back in 1936 a young professional was about to give up the game. He had gone through set after set of clubs, discarding them, chopping and filing at them, always seeking the right clubs. Each time it cost money, something he didn't have in great amounts.

Finally his wife spoke up.

"Why don't you quit kidding yourself," she said. "It can't be entirely the clubs. The trouble must be you."

That, the young pro finally admitted to himself, was it. He had been looking for the perfect set of clubs instead of perfecting his game. He began studying his own swing and that of others. Gradually he developed the swing and sound game which today has made him famous.

His name—Byron Nelson.

You must develop your own game as well. No instructor can blueprint your game. You must know and understand, not only the game of golf, but your own particular game. In this book I have shown you how. If you have followed my teachings carefully, you should have a sound knowledge of the principles.

It is on principles—and in your mind—that your game goes sour. A bad grip can gradually develop in your game if you do not periodically check it. A bad hitch can develop in your swing if you do not, from time to time, go back in your practice sessions to review my formula.

And particularly you can go sour in trying to correct faults. It is most common for golfers to develop a minor fault and, in trying to correct it, actually magnify the error and end up with a serious golfing problem.

In correcting your faults, try to think of your golf swing as a single operation. When you run into golf troubles, try to correct them by first going back through the formula, slowly, step by step.

Use the straight-wrist exercise with first a short backswing, then a slightly longer one, and finally a full backswing. Often you can iron out your difficulties that way with a minimum of danger that new faults will creep in.

Concentration on the fundamentals: grip, stance, weight distribution, hand action, tempo—these are the answers to good golf. And don't forget to swing the club back low at the start of the backswing.

Sometimes your game goes sour during a round of golf. Chick Harbert was just a few strokes off the lead of the Augusta Open as he toured the front 9 in 34. But on the back 9 his game went bad and he took a 47. This type of bad-luck streak, likewise, is going to hit every golfer at some time.

Generally you have to wait out those bad streaks. But sometimes, a quick review of the fundamentals will uncover your trouble in time to save your round.

If, however, you run into a persistent fault that defies self-analysis there is only one sound remedy: consult your pro. The professionals themselves consult other pros not only to improve their game but to correct their golfing faults. Quite often these faults are apparent to the trained observer, but the golfer himself is blind to them.

There are excellent pros in all sections of the country: men like Henry Picard at the Canterbury Country Club, Cleveland; Harry Pressler of San Gabriel, California; Al and Emery Zimmerman of Portland, Oregon; Claude Harmon of Winged Foot, New York; Horton Smith of the Detroit Golf Club and Al Watrous of Oakland Hills in Detroit; Leland Gibson of Blue Hills Country Club, Kansas City—and thousands of other good pros. If you are seriously intent on improving your game, these men can help you.

From time to time review the principles outlined in this book. Briefly stated, my Short Cuts to Better Golf are these:

1. Devote much of your practice time to putting and to your short game. Warm up well before teeing off.

2. In driving and in your wood shots off the fairway, take the proper stance: feet about shoulder width apart, right foot slightly back of the left, knees bent. Waggle, if you can; but in all events get yourself well set. Then swing the club away low and fast. After

the briefest of hesitations, bring the club back down again and strive for a high finish to your follow-through.

3. With the long and medium irons (No. 2, 3, 4, 5, and 6 irons) use the same stance as in driving. The same rules for the swing apply, except that your feet will be closer together.

4. As you get into the scoring zone, you will use the No. 7, 8, or 9 irons and sand iron. Your feet will be closer together than with the longer irons. With these clubs you will use a slightly open stance, left foot slightly back of the right.

5. For chip shots you will use the No. 5, 6, or 7 irons. Although you use the closed stance with the No. 5 and 6 irons ordinarily, for chip shots you will use the slightly open stance. Remember here, as always, to use the crisp quickie rhythm. For both approach and chip shots, let the amount of roll required on the green determine your choice of club. When there is a possible choice, use the club with the least loft.

6. In sand traps use your sand iron, opening up your stance and aiming just behind the ball. Then swing firmly and decisively.

7. From bad lies, play safe above all else. When the ball lies on an upward slope toward the green, shorten your swing, use a club with slightly less loft and aim to the right. For a downhill lie, shorten your swing, aim left, use a club with slightly more loft, and stand a little straighter than usual. With the ball lower than your feet, play the ball off the middle of your stance, take a longer grip on the club, and aim slightly left. When the ball is slightly higher than your feet, shorten your grip, take a short swing, aim a little to the right, and play the ball more off the right foot than normally.

8. Don't forget, for those unusual circumstances, the trick shots: the deliberate hook or slice, the deliberately low-flying or high-flying ball.

9. In putting, check your grip and posture (shoulders, hips parallel to the line of flight, knees bent) and swing the club with a single movement of the arms, hands, and club.

For a more complete review as you may require from time to time, the index at the back of the book will enable you to look up any points on which you are doubtful. Don't be content to read this book once and then put it aside. A periodic review is very important. That's why pupils come back to me year after year for check-ups. You can use this course of lessons in the same way.

From time to time check up on yourself with this quiz:

1. Is your putting grip right?

2. Are you standing and swinging right in your putts?

3. Are you dropping them in consistently with no more than two putts per green?

4. Are your chip shots landing up next to the pin?

5. Are your approach shots hitting the green?

6. Are you getting out of sand traps effectively?

7. Are your iron and wood shots going where you want them to?

8. Are your drives consistently long and accurate?

9. Are you swinging the club away on the backswing?

10. Are you contacting the ball well?

11. Are you following through properly?

12. Are you recovering from bad lies consistently?

13. Is your game staying consistent and, if possible, showing improvement?

The answers to those questions and hundreds more are within the pages of this book. As a final check, fill in score card 9 on the back end leaves.

I have given you, to the best of my ability, a complete picture of golf as I know it. With the aid of pupils from all over the country, I have wr. this book to cover every possible point that may arise in the game.

In closing, I should like to pay special tribute to those who helped me: L. B. Icely, president of Wilson Sporting Goods Company, who offered many helpful suggestions; George S. May of Tam O'Shanter Country Club, to whom every professional is indebted for his untiring efforts to improve tournament golf; Ellsworth Vines, Horton Smith, and dozens of other pros whose assistance simplified the task of compiling this course; the members of the Evanston Golf Club; and to you readers and my other pupils.

I have enjoyed working on this course of lessons for you.

I hope the course has been successful and that through it you have found greater satisfaction, enjoyment, and success in golf.

HANDY PLAYING GUIDE

Drives

Distance (yards)	Club	Comment
225 and up	Driver	Tee up ball. Take shoulder-width stance, slightly closed. Swing the club away low and aim for a slightly inside-out swing.
190	No. 3 wood	Same as driver.
180	" 4, 5 wood	Tee up ball. Feet slightly closer together.
170	" 2 iron	Tee up ball. Slightly closed stance.
160	" 3 "	Same as No. 2 iron. Feet slightly closer together.
150	" 4 "	" " " " " " " " "
140	" 5 "	" " " " " " " " "
130	" 6 "	Same as No. 2 iron. Slightly closed stance, feet slightly closer together for each successive iron.
120	" 7 "	Slightly open stance. Use tee. As in all other shots, play ball off left heel.
100	" 8 "	Same as No. 7 iron.
90	" 9 "	" " " " "

Fairway Shots

Distance (yards)	Club	Lie	Comment
190	No. 3 wood	Normal	Same as drive, except ball is not teed up.
180	" 4, 5 wood	"	Same as No. 3 wood.
170	" 2 iron	"	Same as No. 3 wood. Feet slightly closer together.
160	" 3 "	"	Same as No. 3 wood. Feet slightly closer together.
150	" 4 "	"	Same as No. 3 wood. Feet slightly closer together.
140	" 5 "	"	Same as No. 3 wood. Feet slightly closer together.
130	" 6 "	"	Same as No. 3 wood. Feet slightly closer together.
120	" 7 "	"	Open stance. Feet slightly closer together.

Distance Club (yards)	Lie	Comment
100 " 8 "	"	Open stance. Feet slightly closer together.
90 " 9 "	"	Open stance. Feet slightly closer together.
50 sand iron	"	Open stance. Feet slightly closer together.

Bad Lies

Type of Lie	Comment
Sand	Use sand iron, open stance more, swing naturally, aim slightly back of ball.
Light rough	Use club with slightly more loft than normally.
Heavy rough	Use club with ample loft to get you out of trouble.
Uphill	Shorten swing. Use one less numbered club than normally. Aim right.
Downhill	Shorten swing. Use club with more loft than normally. Stand straighter than usually. Aim left.
Ball lower than feet	Play ball off middle of stance. Take longer grip on club. Aim to left.
Ball higher than feet	Shorten grip. Shorten swing. Aim to right. Play ball off right foot.
Green blocked by trees	Use deliberate hook or slice around obstacle.
Shot blocked by trees	Produce a deliberately low-flying ball. Move hands slightly forward to "hood" club face. Play ball more off right foot. Choke No. 3 or 4 iron.
Shot blocked by trees	Sometimes the answer lies in lofting the ball abnormally high over the hazard. Play ball more off left foot. Take the club back deliberately low so it sweeps the ball into the air.

Approach Shots

Distance from Edge of Green to Pin	Club
Short	No. 9 iron or sand iron
Medium	No. 8 iron
Long	No. 7 iron

Chip Shots

Distance from Edge of Green to Pin	Club	Comment
Short	No. 7 iron	Open stance
Medium	No. 6 iron	" "
Long	No. 5 iron	" "

Putting

Surface	Comment
Flat	Normal Stroke.
On a slope, left to right	Aim slightly to left for slight slope, more to left for pronounced slope.
On a slope, right to left	Aim slightly to the right for slight slope, more for pronounced slope.
Downhill to cup	Loosen grip slightly.
Uphill to cup	Stroke more decisively.
Against the grain	Stroke slightly more decisively.
With the grain	Ease up slightly.
With grain running right to left	Aim slightly right.
With grain running left to right	Aim slightly left.
When confronted with several slopes or, if uncertain as to roll	Aim straight for cup.

INDEX